The Answer Wheel

360 Illuminations for the Human Spirit

Jennifer Darland

Arts of Earth and Sky

ISBN: 979-8-9995355-0-4

The Answer Wheel: 360 Illuminations for the Human Spirit
Arts of Earth and Sky
All text and cover art is original work by Jennifer Darland

This book is dedicated to Kevin, Jack, Logan, and Whitecat,
my Pride and Love

Also by Jennifer Darland

Bridge between Temple and Dream:
Poems from Lonely Nature

Jennifer's Travels
Moonscapes of Recombobulation

The Answer Wheel
360 Illuminations for the Human Spirit

Contents

Introduction

It was summer solstice in the mountains deep inside the woods, my ninth year living off the grid. Tucked in canyon walls, blanketed by the stars, owl and bobcat my witness, it struck with a powerful flash. It was a big question.

What lives inside all of us that everyone can see?

The inspiration was sudden and directive. My quest was to collect and create a Wheel, a 360 degree circle of Answers to explore this question and search for the shared soul essence that lives in all of humanity. Six consecutive evenings of dictation began that very night.

At home in the wilderness, I sat quietly inside an enchanted yurt as the forest darkened around me. Behind closed eyes I found Answers, glimpses into the truth of human perception and experiences recognizable to all people, things that touch us with meaning and transform us, that which gives us courage and rewards us with beauty.

Each night I prepared with a twilight meditation, neutralizing and emptying my mind as much as possible to remain outside of my own ego and personal history. Once I felt clear, a steady flow of imagistic phrases poured from my lips as my scribe penned the words. The orations streamed without pause, spoken in the smooth pace that neither hurries nor hesitates, the scribe's pen always moving, yet too, unrushed. Every word was captured and preserved exactly as said.

While originally I had intended to record ninety Answers four nights in a row, I instead followed the intuitive stopping point that concluded each session. The dictations were complete for the evening when either my thinking mind intervened into the purity of the endeavor or when the natural flow had simply finished its course. I did not keep track of where I was numerically, and nothing about the Wheel was referenced or acknowledged between sessions. My mission was to show up for what turned out to be six nights to collect Answers until my scribe would inform me that I'd spoken the 360th one to complete the Wheel.

As my numerical progress remained a mystery, I did not know it was the last one when I spoke the final Answer. When I did, an oracular authenticity to the work was affirmed. "Lead turns to Gold" is the universal alchemical seal, the ultimate Answer, a perfect completion to the revolution of the Wheel.

A path of greater pursuit opened the way and the Answer Wheel rolled forward to become 360 Illuminations for the Human Spirit, concise passages of insight that further explore and illuminate the essence of each Answer.

The following Readings invite us to imagine and reflect, to inspire meaningful conversation and creative interpretation for a deeper connection to ourselves and others. The Answer Wheel is an invocation to ignite the human spirit and celebrate the roots that connect us, a journey to discover what lives inside all of us that everyone can see.

With love,
Jennifer Darland

2

How to Use the Answer Wheel

Ask a question if you'd like, or let the Answer speak for itself.

Pick a Number

Simply choose a number 1-360 at random, or casually open to any page...

...or, draw from 360 numbered pieces...

The Answer Wheel Deluxe Box Set includes 360 numbered chips along with a draw bag and storage box, available at www.artsofearthandsky.com

Feel free to be creative and craft your own set!

The Interactive Way

Pass the Answer Wheel around for each person to pick a number and read the corresponding message. Let the social magic unfold as every individual has a chance to shine and inspire meaningful conversation to connect the group.

The Quiet Way

Consult intuitively as a personal oracle. A deep reader might consider contemplating one Answer at a time as a focused internal study. However the Wheel is approached, it counsels any inquiry and provides guidance into the beauty and truth of our inner and outer worlds.

Astrological Application

The Wheel can be overlayed upon the Zodiac, aligning the first Answer with the Rising Degree of one's natal chart or the horoscope of any given moment. Counting from here through the Signs leads us to the Answers that correlate with the planetary placements in the chart. If one does not know their birth time, which determines the Rising Degree, or wants to take another look, the first Answer could instead begin from the position of the Sun's Degree, easily located by the birthday or date in question.

For example, if the chart's Rising Degree or Sun Degree is on the cusp of Aries, or 0 Degrees Aries, and the Moon is in 5 Degrees Gemini, the 65th Answer would describe the Moon in this horoscope. To interpret Venus at 7 Degrees Libra, we would seek the 187th Answer. Mars at 27 Degrees Aquarius would lead us to the 327th Answer.

Further Exploration

Be inventive, the Wheel is yours! Make a list of prominent themes in your present stage of life or write a series of your own questions, and pick an Answer for each one. Lay numbers over your favorite Tarot spread. Create your own map to guide an inner quest. Journal how a particular passage applies uniquely to you every day for a week. The Answer Wheel holds potential for endless creative applications and encourages experimentation and novelty.

Enjoy the journey!

The Answers

1. An eagle drops his feather on a windy day

2. Two women stand on a grassy hill and touch fingers

3. A warrior man gallops on a black horse

4. A butterfly sips from a shooting sprout

5. The reflection of the waxing crescent moon is seen in a lake

6. A necklace breaks and a stranger picks it up and fixes it

7. Crickets make music on dewy leaves

8. A mother bird saves her baby from falling

9. A witch's cauldron saves a village with its soup

10. A small child follows two cats into the woods

11. A guardian angel momentarily falls into a lavender bush

12. A nautilus shell washes up at the ocean and reveals a secret

13. A heavy branch falls but many people are spared

14. Two dragonflies race for territory in a thunderstorm

15. Glaciers break into a thousand crystals and flow downstream

16. A hawk flies away with a ten foot snake

17. A band of faeries flies in at midnight and takes away a demon forever

18. A village paints a huge wall while singing

19. A young woman swims out to find a black swan

20. A magic wand is given to a young woman for the first time

21. Sun rays touch the earth and empower a group of young men

22. An elder sees an ultimate truth in a butterfly

23. One hundred shooting stars fall at once

24. In the strangeness of time, one tree grows ten feet in a moment

25. A desperate woman waters her flowers with tears and an unexpected tree bears fruit

26. A panther leisurely hangs his tail from a tree

27. An evil man's weapon is used against him but his son learns

28. A gemstone is passed from one friend to another

29. A raging flood rearranges the atmosphere

30. A pink sunset on a cloud falls as paint

31. A piece of raw evil miraculously turns truly good

32. A joyous couple drinks wine from their own garden

33. A tribe of drummers celebrates with many rhythms

34. Overflowing cups feed the desperate and hungry

35. A clan puts herbs by their ancestor's bones

36. A woman wildly dances in her spirit animal

37. A ship tips over and through jellyfish people survive to shore

38. Laughing people paint themselves in mud

39. A choir sings a sick child to health

40. An old man recovers his heart with a buried treasure box he found

41. Rattles and maracas draw spirits to a bonfire

42. Lightning strikes and a world leader is born

43. An owl makes a nest for his young

44. The strongest people racing through wheat fields

45. Two enemies make peace as they together watch the birth of a fawn

46. A beautiful woman perfects her self portrait

47. A man pounds leather for his family to make clothes

48. An heirloom garden is planted in rich soil

49. A mystic woman bewitches a muggle

50. An instant deluge quells a wildfire

51. A woman blows pollen from her hand and it flies miles

52. The eldest buck escapes his shooter

53. A young class of children is taught timeless wisdom

54. An old sick tree surprisingly bears the finest fruit later

55. Snakes burrow into the sand to save their energy

56. A woman's heartbeat becomes one with a cat's purr

57. In an ecstatic moment a rainbow appears in the sky

58. A tribal woman carves into a boulder

59. A curious child unwinds a spool of thread and rewinds it

60. A man with a sword guides another man into the light

61. A crunch of dry leaves is the only sound under animal's feet

62. Laughing people trade jobs for the day and it goes well

63. A book burner is tossed into the fire and reborn

64. A secret Buddha sheds his grace anonymously

65. A woman makes jewelry to decorate the goddess

66. Under an enchanted tree and aromatic roses lovers kiss

67. People are shivering and then brought freshly cut wool

68. Two dolphins hop the setting sun on the horizon

69. Two squirrels quarrel for nuts but then end up sharing

70. A girl is saved by a bear attack by befriending it

71. Books of myths scattered on tables

72. A long time splinter is removed

73. A woman sits in lotus by a creek

74. An imaginary mermaid saves a believing child

75. Millions of flowers blossom at once all over the world

76. Precious metals have value and meaning

77. Glass breaks but it is remade into something more beautiful

78. Rocky mountains host a religious pilgrimage

79. A group of lepers chant their way to recovery

80. A woman who wove her own robe can escape through thorns

81. Roots of giant trees cool hot feet in the desert

82. A woman hums to charm a snake

83. Shields and arrows fight off invaders

84. A girl passes into womanhood fanned by feathers

85. A giant tortoise peeks from his shell for the first time in years

86. People work together to assemble straw huts

87. Screaming hollers of victory through night insects

88. An egg inside an egg inside an egg

89. A bare foot grasps around a stone

90. Spoonfuls of dark brown honey are the cure

91. A scorpion slides under a drummer's hand unnoticed

92. A parade of animals crosses bridges and gates at night

93. Natural confetti of falling leaves drops in celebration

94. Women paint each other's faces in the moonlight

95. A warm morning breakfast at a cold icy farm

96. Thunder shakes broken musical instruments back to life

97. A butterfly lays its delicate legs on the thorn

98. A long metal vessel of sacrificial herbs

99. The ceiling and rug are exactly the same in a holy place

100. A spirit in the sky is actually jumping stars

101. Clams clipping barnacles from the toxins of the sea

102. Dancing freely in a spinning dress at dawn

103. Bows and arrows striking marks on trees

104. The moment an injured dog knows it will be okay and walks again

105. A foolish one gets deeply lost in a cave

106. A child walks up stairs in a public building for a life duty

107. Howling wolves break a long time silence

108. A young woman dives off a cliff and hits her head but it's not that bad

109. A string of bells for miles chimes all at once

110. Pouring bubbly drinks makes it sticky

111. An electric lightbulb fades in and out

112. A naked tribe walks through grasses taller than they are

113. A panicked man is hollering and no one can hear him

114. A woman walks alone in night streets singing

115. A woman gives birth in a bed of flowers

116. A total blackness without even one starlight in the sky

117. Tiny birds flying over vast oceans

118. The boot is ripped on the fence while running by

119. Two lovers trace each other's palm lines

120. Ecstatic people dance with shadows

121. Someone levitates from a singing chorus

122. The lizard runs in circles drawing spirals in the sand

123. A luxurious hammock is swinging but nobody is in it

124. A woman lying on her back as a spirit comes down to kiss her

125. A globe spins as someone searches for answers

126. Everyone is laughing at the mockery in the middle of the room

127. All of the angels descend into human beings for a brief effective moment

128. Hot metal sits heating in hot coals

129. Hiker adventures are covered in pine sap

130. He steps over the hole of death but only sprains his ankle

131. A hungry shark heads to shore

132. Demons break up a worship ceremony but cannot get it

133. A musical genius composes their first piece

134. A saw cuts off the source of splinters

135. An anchor drops to the deepest point of the ocean

136. A comet restores faith in a hopeless teenager

137. A treehouse amongst cliffs holds stacks of books and a fireplace

138. A ring of people hold hands to guard a castle

139. Water evaporates and invisible life drinks from it

140. A child picks flowers for someone they bullied

141. A small needle is lost forever in sand

142. A plume of worrisome smoke turns out to be sacred smudge

143. A pine cone falls and has a strangely long tumble down an endless hill

144. Fluffy clouds host the real believer

145. Women weave curtains for privacy from men

146. A wild dog attack chases someone up a tree otherwise impossible to climb

147. A woman hangs upside down for a new perspective

148. A magician teaches a rare disciple

149. A mad person ties and unties knots

150. A beach at night lit with rows of candles

151. Dry skin is quenched with bee balm

152. Young boys race each other laughing

153. A mystic briefly sees the laws of the universe

154. An evolved reincarnation comes for a good person

155. A butterfly escapes a spiderweb in the nick of time

156. Sea salt rubs away weeping poison

157. Gardeners sift compost with their hands

158. A mother tells her child to make a wish

159. A pocket too heavy breaks open

160. A champion of peace sends a message in a bottle

161. A woman at the peak of her beauty ties her hair back

162. A love letter is written but they get a paper cut

163. Wild animals running freely on open plains

164. A holder of wisdom writes down secrets

165. A young warrior is ceremoniously pierced

166. Old wooden wheels stuck in asphalt

167. Curious people sort out rocks, shells, and fossils

168. Ink is spilled and something beautiful is created

169. A pensive inventor ponders the next move

170. A magnifying glass skims over a globe

171. A family finds joy juicing berries with their hands

172. Blue birds land on a tiny island no one knows about

173. Two sticks finally spark a fire after a long time

174. A scalpel removes a deadly growth

175. A girl speaks promises out loud as she braids her hair

176. A window rusted shut breaks open

177. A long fishing line cast off a tall balcony

178. Two evils burn each other out in a fight

179. A god designs a new bush of spices

180. A child first discovers their spirit animal in a dream

181. Two people pulling bundles uphill with ropes

182. A peaceful woman wrestles with a ghost

183. A rock wedged into a tree opening

184. A gold coin flipped

185. Pounding mallets to build structures

186. White ashes spread by the wind

187. Curtains fall, a naked woman in the window

188. A girl brushes and saddles her horse for a long journey

189. A wanderer finds their place and becomes a hermit

190. A witch coven meets at midnight

191. Autumn leaves turning color

192. The top story of a house falls

193. Dungeon doors snap open

194. A group of people lost in a maze

195. A man tries to stop a wheel from spinning but can't

196. Mushroom mycelium mixing with tree roots

197. A waterfall builds stacks of foam

198. One with too much on his back sets some of it down

199. Two fruit trees grow twisted around each other

200. A non-receiver accepts a gift

201. A girl stubs her toe when she is off to the wrong adventure but then is set right

202. A pile of empty cocoons

203. Treasures are collected for a beloved elder

204. A swamp dries up to receive fresh rain

205. Friends cut up photographs and rearrange them

206. A man on a mountain sits still and breathes

207. A tiger chases a rabbit

208. A writer rips up her pages and starts over

209. A spider rolls up a wasp that is larger

210. A shaky hand holds a roll of keys searching for the one to fit the keyhole

211. Moths glowing in the dark at night

212. A thick layer of ice hardens the earth

213. A baby feeds from its mother for the last time

214. Trees fall horizontal in a windstorm

215. A joyous and beautiful funeral

216. Women making cups and bowls on a riverbank

217. Crystal clear water in a bowl of pink granite on a mountaintop

218. Bats flying low to the ground in the evening

219. An army sharpens iron weapons

220. A crane lands by a bathing woman

221. Workers clear a cluttered road

222. A spell worker learns how to become invisible

223. A woman stares intently into a mirror

224. The full moon shines light on a celestial storm

225. An alter of gemstones from all over the world

226. An ancient seed unlikely sprouts

227. A band playing beautiful music underwater

228. Someone of long bad luck suddenly becomes lucky

229. A primitive medicine person sews wild stitches

230. A community chants for its well being

231. A poacher gets turned on and killed by his own attack

232. Wild animals graze on land where no humans have ever been

233. A tense cloud in the atmosphere breaks free

234. An earthquake creates a divide

235. Footsteps crush vegetation but it springs up again

236. A snake catches a mouse but then a hawk gets them both

237. A house of people are rapt by a charismatic speaker

238. A crystal ball splashes into water at the bottom of a well

239. A young hero is anointed

240. A group of gamblers shuffle cards

241. A volcano erupts and static electricity runs rampant

242. A fisherman's net captures a school of fish

243. Igloos melt at the fire breath of a dragon

244. A woman finds shelter from a hailstorm underground

245. A tribe climbs trees to harvest acorns

246. A tricked man is chained out of his own house

247. The scales of an injured reptile shimmer iridescence in the sun

248. Two magnets inch together from opposite ends of the earth

249. An owl leads home a lost child

250. A naïve youth resists seduction

251. A villain shakes bottles of bubbling poison

252. Tangled copper wires clutter a space

253. A mist suspends life in midair

254. Skeletons dance around in secret when no one is looking

255. A dead beast is skinned for leather

256. A starved woman ravages smoked meat from a bone

257. An abandoned baby is found crying in a carriage

258. A self-loving woman adorns herself with butter and wax

259. Two different plants cross-pollinate into something new

260. An enormous pendulum is hypnotizing its watchers

261. Clothes worn in battle are washed and whipped dry in the wind

262. Plagues of locust come for the grain but for the first time men storm them away

263. A man dodges a fatal sword strike by inches

264. Dead souls cross the veil and come to life for a day

265. A sorcerer dreams of a tiger claw and really finds it

266. A sharp fanged beast breaks up a crowd

267. The only humans with stones as eyes find one another

268. A mangled path is cleared of debris

269. Two women read tea leaves together

270. A dedicated one masters their art

271. A healer grinds spices and barks with a mortar and pestle

272. Two ancient warring families make peace

273. A stampede suddenly breaks from pure silence

274. A crackling fire spits sparks

275. The wind changes direction quickly many times

276. A huge glass bottle fit for a giant is dug up in the sand

277. Tiny footprints found in deep dark caves

278. Determined scribes hurriedly scribbling

279. A small child covers an elder with a blanket

280. Rich syrup is squeezed from leaves of a tree

281. A man and a woman hang upside down together

282. A treasured vase breaks into a thousand jewels

283. Meager grains are pounded to relieve famine

284. Hard ground is broken up to receive life

285. A crystal on a crystal on a crystal that grows every direction

286. A totem pole collapses and a new one is built

287. A belly dancer hands sea shells to a crowd

288. Roses grow up around a cross

289. Fruit sap drops down layers of trees

290. A religious expedition is led by a torch into the night

291. Burned desert feet are relieved by a boulder's shadow

292. Women trade strings and beads

293. Lovers taste dew on the morning grass

294. A woman mixes water and clay

295. A rainbow hits glass and turns into prisms

296. One's eyes turn inward and they can see

297. A big leaf holds a pattering of water

298. A fox enters new territory for the first time

299. A magic woman turns into flower petals as she walks away

300. A chained up man is released

301. Dark birds peck into the earth

302. People draw symbols in the dirt with their toes

303. A pure spirit is born and a demonic one dies

304. A group of masters meet the true master

305. The ill are soothed with barks and boiling water

306. An uninhabited island goes underwater

307. Children skipping rocks on a lake

308. A lush pond with algae and croaking frogs

309. A clairvoyant benefits from a séance

310. A vampire drinks blood and then dies

311. A god makes an appearance for his people

312. A flock of birds lands in a park for scattered grains

313. A bridge is built from two sides

314. Numb walking souls come to life

315. A high mountain peak where spirits take form

316. Deep in the wilderness a solo explorer draws on cliffs with charcoal

317. A rich meal is cooked after a sporting victory

318. A rebellious spirit rejects her pre-prescribed path

319. A lone wolf howls at the moon

320. An ecstatic woman rises into the sky

321. A band of thieves rides wagons in the night

322. A generous family hosts greedy visitors

323. A man and a woman carry logs to a wood stove

324. A long scroll unrolls with a never before read story

325. A hardened person softens as they break down and cry

326. A sweep of bravery inspires a coward to take a daring quest

327. A lion outruns its enemy

328. A mother finds her lost child

329. A hungry bear emerges from long hibernation

330. The subtle rise and fall of the heart is observed on a loved one's chest

331. A group chants and prays and it all comes true

332. Night bugs fly into a candle and die

333. A small space in the earth rests a weary traveler

334. Willpower forbids an insistent parasite

335. A book of knowledge illuminates a seeker

336. A strong force suddenly collects many magnets

337. Behind a dark veil a dark elf nature spirit guards a secret pond

338. A storm destroys a house but it is built back stronger

339. An orphan learns meaning and heritage

340. A large first harvest from a sacred garden

341. A cobra slides between two thrones

342. An old man and old woman stare at each other wide-eyed

343. A lovely woman caresses her own skin

344. A spiral makes a black hole in the sky

345. Escaped pearls gather on the ocean floor

346. An old elk lays down to feed a village

347. Exiled people find some place even better

348. A dark phantom of night breaks into the day

349. Artists pound and chisel sculpted bone

350. Women fix feathers into each other's hair

351. A high domed ceiling hosts echoes of sermons

352. A child breaks through an icy lake but lives

353. The full moon illuminates an owl perched on a tree

354. A mystic has her first psychic vision

355. Confidantes whispering secrets in each other's ears

356. A distant war recedes and the residents cheer

357. A victory speech that inspires as champagne is poured

358. The sounds of celestial bodies become pleasantly perceptible for a brief moment

359. The hot ash grows a secret flower

360. Lead turns to gold

The Readings

1. An eagle drops his feather on a windy day

A majestic creature of the sky, the great eagle soars respectfully in the heavenly space above us. The windy day is stirring up energies, directions are shifting and new inspirations and insights are gusting through the airy spaces of potential around us. Blustering ideas and meddled thoughts could perplex us early in the day, but when we expose ourselves and face the winds, we receive the message of the eagle as a spiritual guide. In these whirlwinds of change, the fallen feather delivers an enlightening clue. If we accept the feather as an offering and open up to its ascended abode, we connect to a higher principle that allows communication with a greater spirit. We trust the keen sight of the powerful eagle and feel the lightness of the feather asking us to rise.

2. Two women stand on a grassy hill and touch fingers

The vibrancy of two women together evokes mysterious connection and intimacy. We imagine a mirrored double beauty the women recognize and bring to life in one another, a mutual reflection of the feminine divine. By touching each other's fingertips they share a delicate interaction of heart, a reciprocated empowerment. Upon the grassy hill where they stand we feel uplifted and positive, in a position to praise and be praised. The women and the sloped grasses emanate a liveliness, a healthy mount from where we may gaze and honor the fertile world around us. There is a gentle but pristine activation at play, the intuitive feminine power sparked to life. We are moved to acknowledge and embrace the female energy alive in ourselves and the women around us from this exalted point of honor and appreciation.

3. A warrior man gallops on a black horse

The warrior man on a galloping horse is charged with dynamism, speed, and virility, the ultimate yang force. A strong masculine hero is present and ready for a challenge, and he is quite capable. The urgency of opposition is gaining tension, something is ready for swift confrontation. There is an immediate need to either assert or defend, and we hope the rider is righteous in his endeavor, that the call of duty is honorable. The black horse could suggest a dark energy involved, so caution is advised as we proceed with this momentum. Equipped with the necessary stamina and emboldened to succeed in the triumph at hand, we ride in with the balanced attitude of a true warrior to achieve a virtuous win.

4. A butterfly sips from a shooting sprout

A butterfly is among the most stunning beauties in existence, visually spectacular in form and movement, profound in transformation. The iridescent colors symmetrically lined and dotted across each wing, their light and easy flight, the way they glide and land on the liveliness of a shooting sprout, the grace of their every move. A finesse of sweetness wisps by in the short flutter of this succulent sip. It is time to savor the nectar of fresh potential budding with life and focus on a new possibility of becoming. We should saturate ourselves with juices of revival, noticing and drinking in the beauty around us, what holds the power to renew and fortify, to quench our thirst for what we desire. A crisp sapling offers a burst of growth, a new journey blessed by the butterfly, a visitation of celestial wings.

5.   The reflection of the waxing crescent moon is seen in a lake

The waxing moon is the phase of increasing energy, expanding what was seeded at the new moon. Our current objects of focus and intention have yet to reach their full expression. The crescent shape indicates the gestation is in its early stages, absorbing and accelerating influences that will affect its eventual culmination. The growing moon is not in direct sight, but is a reflection on a lake, moonlight cast on the water as our well of emotions, revealing the need to implore our emotional contents, to shine light on the depths of our own watery stillness. Once we enter the lake and pierce the reflection, we breach the sheen of illusion and become aware of what lurks beneath our own dark waters, and then cleansed we look up to the moon and receive its full illumination. In the light of the moon we observe the cycles that habitually wax and wane in our lives, the ripples of light that perpetually rise and fall, the deep lake as our emotional body, the hidden surface of all experience.

6. A necklace breaks and a stranger picks it up and fixes it

Necklaces are made of jewels and metals, conductors of energy, transmitters used to attract or dispel, amulets that often hold personal meaning. As the necklace breaks, its energy is unclasped, disrupted, and though at first we experience a loss, we soon learn the damaged pieces are salvageable. The solution appears unexpectedly, a stranger stops to fix the necklace. The fragmented pieces are instantly restored after this voluntary act of kindness, the scattered intention of our adornment is whole again, the broken thread of beauty is cherished once more thanks to the generosity of the passerby. Whatever breaks need not be ruined, especially when we are open to receiving and providing charitable solutions outside the familiar comfort of what we already know.

7. Crickets make music on dewy leaves

The song of crickets is a supernaturally soothing natural ambiance, sacred as the angelic choir of the living forest. Their synchronized chorus pulses the mystery of a common rhythm, singing together as one grand coordination of hypnotic sound, a living, breathing, atmospheric harmony. The settling of night's etheric waters falls as dew, the benediction of morning, lush leaves and celestial sound greeting the heavenly dawn of light. An enchanted energy has delivered the day with charmed promise, the tempo of a living magic that connects all existence. A moment to beat together as one, we discover ourselves within the natural mystical throb of everything, and brought through the night with the crickets' song we awaken, serenaded still into this verdant morning.

8. A mother bird saves her baby from falling

The mother has nested and nurtured her baby, a natural bond so attuned she is able to save the fledgling from its fall. Though no harm was done, the great leap was taken too soon, the eager must be patient to avoid catastrophe. As mother, extra attention is needed to keep an eye on the untried as the young test their wings for the first time, ready to catch them if they fall. Risks are necessary to move onward and upward, we throw ourselves into real-life situations to assess our readiness, the bird evidently not yet strong enough to fly away. Another increment of incubation in the safety of the nest under a more experienced wing will strengthen and teach the young bird, who in the near future will be ready as ever to fly into its own fate. When the time arrives, the supportive mother releases her attachment, the availability of her immediate rescue and, no longer dependent, the capable offspring flies free, the maternal bond intact from afar.

9. A witch's cauldron saves a village with its soup

The witch's cauldron bubbles with a purposeful potion of simmering broth, each ingredient intentionally selected from her apothecary, whatever she has summoned from her spell books and stores of recipes that span the wide spectrum of good and evil. This soup is infused by an apparently good witch, her tonic has induced a healing that saves an entire village. Something magical has been brewing, an invocation for a greater good has manifested on the material plane from the invisible world. The witch's stew has churned the workings of a benevolent spell, the preparation in the cauldron is fully cooked, charged up and ready to dish out its healing magic, a pot of plenty for the village to share, grateful for the local witch and her concoction.

10. A small child follows two cats into the woods

A natural magnetic pulls the small child to the edge of the forest, and lured by two cats, enters its wild beauty. The child sets off from a place of innocence, and lacking any real experience, there are lessons to learn along the way. To thrive, the young explorer must smell and listen to the intricacies of their surroundings, to enter the forest not blindly but alert as the all-seeing eye of the cat. With the cat as our guide we exhibit stealth and agility as we find our way through the woods, sure-footed, composed, and acutely aware. We learn to step with a gentle and confident precision that circumvents danger, remaining ready to pounce when it comes time for the hunt. Two cats suggest a duality, contrasting forces may tug us in different directions, but with the sharp clarity of the graceful feline we sense the subtleties that will lead us the right way. Embodying the deliberate strength of the vigilant cat, we are poised to succeed in this brave call to adventure, revolutionizing ourselves in this wild hunt for the soul.

11. A guardian angel momentarily falls into a lavender bush

A guardian angel is a godly messenger from the heavenly realm who personally protects and guides their respective individual mortal being with whom they are partnered on earth. Our angelic counterpart appears to us now in this brief aromatic flash of lavender, an herb that comforts and soothes, a sensory relief offered from the heavens if we can identify this divine visitation as a compassionate ally that transpires into the physical on our own behalf. With our mystical guardian present there is a restoration of faith, a solace that alleviates our troubles, a spiritual entity that can feel into our beings and console us. This arrival offers correspondence with a living spiritual sentience as a piece of ourselves. A blessing has manifested from a vital mystery on the other side, and our faith is surging after we are gifted with this holy company.

12. A nautilus shell washes up at the ocean and reveals a secret

A shell rolls up on the tide to reveal a secret, an intimate feminine essence is ready to be shared. The shell, born of the ocean, has been surfed and scrubbed with salt to clean her before she washes up to shore in this moment of unfolding. Vulvic and dense with birth and sex and life, the feminine is open, a private piece of herself breathing in the open air, a sensual exposure of secret knowing. She rides in the waves of perfect beautiful form as the sacred golden ratio of the nautilus, the growth pattern of petals and spirals, leaves and animals, the organic proportion as the code to all creation. The watery rhythm of feminine nature, perfect timing as the tide of the ocean and the depths of woman, the shell of the sea as her sacred emblem, her treasure trove, her sea of secrets, the ocean bliss we all adore.

13. A heavy branch falls but many people are spared

With the combination of good luck and awareness of our environment, we can escape the crash of the heavy branch. The looming threat has fallen from above so a scan of what lies overhead is prudent to avoid ominous aftershocks. It is important to avoid seeing probable doom in everything, but simultaneously remain cognizant of our surroundings and recognize the potential dangers around us. Pondering the reality of luck and chance, we consider that correct orientation of ourselves in relation to a given situation will likely lead us to more fortunate outcomes. At the same time, we ultimately accept we have little to no control over inevitable random events that are part of reality, knowing that we do however have great influence over what we attract into our lives and how we react to our circumstances.

14. Two dragonflies race for territory in a thunderstorm

These competing dragonflies zip through contested territory, masters of aerial acuity winding through shortcuts and speeding by labyrinths, fast tight turns and attention to detail essential as they fly through the crashing rain in this mad dash to the finish. The thunderstorm intensifies this race for the win, loud booms and lightning, the noisy scene riveting and exciting. Electricity snaps through the air, the duel is on in the stormy nebulous that will grant victory somewhere within the dynamism of lights and thunder. This competition is a tiny piece of a wider storm, all part of the grand display, each small sight majestic and important when noticed. With rapid accuracy and magnified perspective our competitive spirit flies with a thunderous bang in this wet and wild race!

15. Glaciers break into a thousand crystals and flow downstream

Glaciers are the reservoirs of life, our purest waters preserved in these solid storehouses of frozen potential. With no signs of melting, the break is not ubiquitous in all glaciers but selective as though struck by a hammer of the gods. A cascade of positive energy is released as the ice transforms into a thousand crystals and flows downstream to energize and bless the world. Rigidity ruptures and a fresh life force cracks open, crystalline abundance spills forth to relieve stagnation, latent powers gain momentum and accessibility in this distribution of vision and possibility. As we enjoy the refreshment of this new vitality, the stores at the top of the fountain must meanwhile be replenished to ensure the glacial reserves are protected for the future, a source from which later riches may bless us again.

16. A hawk flies away with a ten foot snake

The majesties of earth and sky are united as the winged serpent. Though the beautiful predator of the sky has hunted the snake, a

31

terrestrial mirror of his prowess, the capture illustrates a primordial image of the sacred connection between heaven and earth. The hawk gives wings to the sensuous earthly body while the long energy spiral of the earth-charged snake gives striking capacity to the winged beast. Together they ascend into the firmament, ten feet as a measured completion, a circuit of infinity. The dexterous skill of the hawk has marked its earthly victory as the snake rises into the heavens, the ruler of the cold blooded underworld now feathered and flying. A powerful flight of consciousness has departed into the clouds in this mystical symbol of divine understanding.

17. A band of faeries flies in at midnight and takes away a demon forever

The band of faeries is from a magical realm, a layer of life beyond the ordinary eye. They secretly arrive in the black sheath of midnight, private and away from the light where they grapple with a malevolent force lurking in the darkness. Whether this evil is tucked within our own subconscious as a disturbance within ourselves, or operates as a disruptive inferno in the outer world, the banishment is final and therefore heavily significant. A frequency of goodness from a dimension of existence we cannot perceive with our sight has driven this diabolical energy away, where a portal opens to cast off our hellish enemies of fear and discord into permanent exile. We are freed from something demonic that will no longer possess us after this major triumph of supernatural intervention.

18. A village paints a huge wall while singing

A cherished tribal moment is shared in this communal project, the creative spirit alive and singing during this inspired renovation, the implementation of sound further sensationalizing each brushstroke. Village morale is greatly enhanced, a renewed presentation for the community is put on display for everyone to enjoy, the voices and visions of many souls imbued into the fresh paint spread across the huge wall. The sharpened energy and color will continue to uplift the residents and all who pass by the mural each day, where the joy of the artists' collective expression will continue to ring, as art carries with it the moods and feelings felt during its creation, all captured in the spirit of the image. Imagining this inspirited art, we are led to consider what existing platforms around us are ready to be remodeled into something joyous and beautiful, an aesthetic gift to our community we can contribute with the exhilarated enthusiasm of communal rapport.

19. A young woman swims out to find a black swan

The young woman swims out to explore new waters, to immerse herself in a fresh sea of experience. She clearly seeks deviation from the norm in her search for the black swan, and though there are general predictabilities in life standard to all events and people, such as the assumption boats and aquatic life will be on the waters, the margin of expectation paradoxically still including surprises and chaos, the anomaly itself becoming our course of reason is something that cannot be planned. As the woman finds the odd discovery of the black swan has become her destination, she realizes the fallacy of

33

conclusive thought systems that suspend us in disbelief, stuck at the shore fearing remote waters of the disillusioned impossible. Whatever we set out to find in this expedition will reveal an unexpected irregularity, a decisive event that eludes all rationalization, likely to shift the paradigm completely and alter our life moving forward in a most unpredictable way.

20. A magic wand is given to a young woman for the first time

The magical ability to cast charms is bequeathed in this initiation. Receiving the wand puts direct power into the young woman's hands, she is granted access to conduct energy in supernatural worlds. A commencement into a higher place, this comes with tremendous responsibility for the wielder of the wand, who now, with study and practice, can influence and function within advanced planes of magic, and hence must remain strong-willed to avoid corruption. This is a life-altering rite of passage, an evolution from the limitations of ordinary thought perspectives into larger thinking that encompasses and allows space for bigger outcomes. If we work the powers of our will and mind to integrate with the magical conductions of the wand, we are amazed to see we can shape reality more than we might think. Matured and proficient to use the new wand bestowed, this is a great privilege of special power, if discipline is practiced and we are wise enough to keep it.

21. Sun rays touch the earth and empower a group of young men

A divine presence touches this group of young men through a solar outreach. Sunrays as the source and sustainer of all life pour into the men, a youthful brotherhood growing into fathers and warriors, ready to assert their life giving forces into the receptive beings that are prepared to be warmed by this solar touch. The torch of the sun has been handed to us and we are equipped to venture forth and assert our active principles of self. This moment is beyond the hue of normal every day light, and it reaches much further. For the sunrays to touch earth and strike the young men with such direct potency, we can realize that we are supported by the deific bounty that lives in this grand frequency of godly visitation. Strength has arrived and we are vigorous, our dream is in arm's reach, now what shall we do with this power at hand?

22. An elder sees an ultimate truth in a butterfly

Elders have vast accumulations of life experience, their inner contents of reflections and understandings reach far and wide. The elder's vision of ultimate truth in a butterfly conveys the simple elegance of what is best treasured in life. The beauty of the butterfly and its wondrous transformations brings the stillness of revelation in the exquisite mysteries that surround us. This moment of observation teaches us that the purity of truth is discovered in the details we choose to notice. The existence of truth is elusive, it may land for a moment in a temporary form of profound insight and then fly back into the great unknown. Whispers of knowing as fleeting inspirations are here one moment and then disappear, keeping us in a perpetual flight of wonder, as with the wise elder who continues to seek new truth.

23. One hundred shooting stars fall at once

Many monads of rare occurrence disperse simultaneously, a supremely auspicious moment that opens a quick window where unique energies are aligned. The normally erratic nature of shooting stars flashing in their individual rhythms ceases and one hundred of them fall at the same time. A strange synchronicity, a break away from the ordinary leaves us astonished as this lucky encounter lights up the night sky. As the macrocosm reveals this universal charm blinking like many eyes opening all at once, we sense that the magic is also seeing us, rather than only ourselves seeing the magic. If we can attune to this momentary access of marvelous coincidence, perhaps whatever we contribute within our own microcosms during this quick flash will shine brighter and with more potency. This propitious timing suggests that a brief moment of unusual opportunity is available now, and if we have open eyes and a gaze astute enough to catch it, a special moment is here to enchant and contradict what may otherwise seem impossible.

24. In the strangeness of time, one tree grows ten feet in a moment

One tree growing ten feet in an instant compels us to understand this as an extraordinary period, when much is accomplished in a short while. A rapid growth spurt is occurring, we are fully embodied in the developmental domain. Great progress is made with swiftness and ease, and we are so occupied that time is irrelevant. In another light we can read this as many years of tree growth sped by and we didn't even notice, time was not spent with full awareness of the incremental changes around us that make life fascinating. In either case, we should remember to enjoy the things slowly changing and growing, to not let the moments of quality time slip by, and instead soak up the natural richness of every moment, if only in the passive act of observation. If we move too fast the phases of life will hustle by us, yet there are periods of great activity when we are energized to grow ten feet in a moment. Engaging in a balance of active and passive energy in the minutes that endlessly tick by is to discover the art of perfect timing.

25. A desperate woman waters her flowers with tears and an unexpected tree bears fruit

A desperate woman's distress has shattered into tears, a despair so heavy that her weeping is abundant enough to water her flowers. By freely unleashing her emotions and letting herself cry, the burden of her immense sorrow flows away and nourishes the plants around her. As the forest feeds on what is dead to us, so too do our difficult emotions fuel the latent beauty and life that is yet to bloom around us. This image teaches us that if we allow the emotional process to fulfill itself, the difficult times are temporary, and if we can channel the energy towards something beneficial, it has the ability to transform into a positive force. May we never repress our sadness, but instead pour it into something beautiful such as an earthly nurturing, love for another, or a creative work of art. If we can express our emotions in a healthy way, we are able to transmute pain into the spirit of fecundity where an unexpected tree bears fruit.

26. A panther leisurely hangs his tail from a tree

In the leisurely energy of the wild panther we feel a satiated coolness in this elevated respite, lifted and supported by what must be a mighty tree. The tail speaks volumes in the act of the cat, its soft swing indicating a smooth feeling of mellow confidence and satisfaction. Apparently free of hurry and immediate need, we are wildly comfortable in our sleek panther animal self, our robust muscular body part of naked nature in peaceful connection with the tree. In this passing gift of pure enjoyment may we fully indulge in the pleasure of simply existing and slip into the calm easy swing of the leisurely cat gazing from its jungle heights. This is a moment to hang out and observe and rest until we are ready to jump off the tree in wild pursuit once again.

27. An evil man's weapon is used against him but his son learns

A wielder of evil himself has been hit by the backfire of his own strike. This exhibits the inevitable truth that all the myriad nuances we emit, intentions grand and small, will attract and connect with like energies that will return to us the same qualities we have projected. The image is ultimately redemptive, an evil force intercepted by the virtue of the young man who has learned. The slate of malice has been wiped clean, the weapon's evil is overthrown and halted by knowledge, a refusal of generational continuity by a man's own son. A cord of transference has been cut in this youthful wisdom that has chosen to reject the evil force that may have otherwise corrupted him. A state of hope is restored as we are reminded that we must pay careful attention to the energetic dynamics we both propagate and absorb, knowing that whatever we perpetuate is sure to return our way.

28. A gemstone is passed from one friend to another

The inherent characteristics of the gemstone are further amped up by accumulation of human story, here absorbing the spirit of friendship as it is passed along as a gift. Precious stones are composed from raw natural elements of the earth, holding powers that can repel or attract unseen potentials, thereby affecting our personal experiences especially when kept physically or sentimentally close to us. Every gemstone carries a unique charge and set of energetic properties, a composition that is the result of both what is intrinsic to the stone as well as what its piezoelectric lattices have accrued along the way from our personal psychic contributions. As we pass this jewel on to a friend we are conscious of the energies travelling with it, offering us a chance to charge it up with good intentions and positive vibrations that will remain in the stone for the benefit of our friend, and wherever else it may journey in the future.

29. A raging flood rearranges the atmosphere

Raging waters are among the strongest physical forces in our world, something intense is happening here. Floodwaters have completely rearranged the atmosphere and we must brace ourselves for significant change. The context of heavy waters could indicate substantial emotional involvement as a piece of this rampage, yet we must remember that though catastrophes can feel overwhelming at the time, they do not necessarily result in permanent devastation. Often forcefully imposed changes eventually turn out to be instigators of much needed renewal, working in favor of our environments or ourselves by washing out toxic or stagnant energies that no longer serve the space. In any case, it is a time to be resilient and accommodating to the inevitable changes. It is a good idea to determine where we best stand in this new arrangement and optimize the shifting variables that will fall in place as the stabilizing elements of our new situation.

30. A pink sunset on a cloud falls as paint

The beauty of the pink sunset with its cloud sliding by erupts with a sensuous aesthetic as dripping paint blurs the line in our mind between imagination and reality. In our inspired reverie we can almost see a sheet of sun kissed silk slipping from a pink lined cloud to fall wet onto our canvas, splashing pink paints warm to the touch. Intimations of orange burst into the vision as the brushstrokes sweep a frenzy of creation. We are artistically stimulated in this picture, absorbed in this flight of beauty where we are free to wander in our own creative space. As the curtains of the day close we feel

40

comfortable and cozy, a sense of peace falls and calls us to relax into our visions. The magic of the evening requests we release our worldly inhibitions and surrender to the wonder of this marvelous sky, where we look up and paint with the joyous and colorful life of dream and imagination.

31. A piece of raw evil miraculously turns truly good

This is a deep rooted victory where an honest good supersedes a true evil, a rawness we sense springing directly from source. We can feel this evil vessel, this tangible piece the image puts in our hands. We are empowered to touch this fragment of consciousness and hold it so that we may observe it and help guide it towards the fields of goodness. A spark of divine support enters the picture with the inclusion of the word miraculous, revealing a genuine and powerful truth in the turn towards benevolence. With our orientation near a point of raw origins, the early effects of this positive change will likely flow far into future evolutions with this causal momentum. We consider what might be held in the clench of evil so that we may loosen its grasp and, unshy of a miracle, we can replenish those spaces with that which is heartful and good.

32. A joyous couple drinks wine from their own garden

A joyous union shown in many dedicated phases of cooperation and patience has been sustained to achieve this satisfactory result of making wine with home grown grapes. Perseverance and hard work were maintained to earn this celebratory moment, from creating the garden in the first place to planting the seed and nurturing the plant to fruition, all before the further wait to actually ferment the grapes into wine. This is a sequence of many stages that build upon each other and must endure the test of time. We begin within ourselves to establish a sincere loving foundation for earth and home allowing us to cultivate our gardens and find harmony with our partners in love and life. As we enjoy the bounty of what we've grown, may we be enriched by these sips of our spirits as our happiness progresses into productive momentum with ongoing fertility and abundance in the gardens of our lives.

33. A tribe of drummers celebrates with many rhythms

This gathering of drums evokes a primal humanity that beats inside all of us in this tribal celebration. We've lit the grooves that wait quiet inside until the sleeping beast awakens in the wild raps of rhythm enlivened by drum and dance. With these depths brought alive we move with our people, a communal soul unleashed free into the bones of these beats that move us in this ravish of sound and feeling. We are carried to the sacred world as travelled by the sound of drum and set loose to the music. Our tribal hearts moving as one in this celebratory wave, we are pulled from our worries into the beating heart of the clan. Inside the living pulse we are liberated to explore the freedom of our own individual expressions, to reach our fullest private souls that wish to move and flourish, beyond the throbs of our warm blood that longs to dance wild. We bend into this living plasma of rhythmic sound allowing the truest nature of our visceral selves to awaken in the mutual love of the shared music.

34. Overflowing cups feed the desperate and hungry

A time of prosperity where cups are filled and abundance spills forth to feed the desperate and hungry. The watery element that delivers the image gives the passage a flowing quality that is easy and nongrasping. Such bounty tells us the cup that provides is sturdy and full so the surplus is not strenuous but natural. Whether of work or energy or food or money, there is excess to be shared in a pleasant outpour of generosity. If we find our own cups empty and feel too dry to give, this abundance of time or wealth can be directed towards what is starving in the self, and meanwhile we can scan to see what value we find within by which others might be fed. We are called to let the waters flow, reservoirs of life are plenty and ready to pour into thirsty domains.

35. A clan puts herbs by their ancestor's bones

A call to honor heritage, from parents to legendary ancestors of long ago it is a moment to respect our lineage. Each of us has a long strand of complex historical roots, a thread touched by many generations full of spirits that infused the life force in our blood with their earlier imprints. Every familial cord has nurtured successions of bodies and souls into fruition, giving us background and beginning for who we are, providing the foundations of our being. With this presentation of herbs we acknowledge a member of our clan who lived long ago with reverence and gratitude for what we have received along this long line, realizing that it had to unfold exactly as

43

it did for us to have birthed into this existence at all. This sacramental herbal offering is a gesture to sanctify the ancestral spirits whose eternal influence affects living lineages, an earthly veneration of the line that continues to live as a piece of ourselves.

36. A woman wildly dances in her spirit animal

The exuberant wild feminine is freed in this ecstatic dance, autonomous and released of human confines she is liberated in this journey of animal spirit. Her earthly self is unharnessed from societal behavior and she is roaming in her animalistic delights. Shifting in and out of furs and scales, we become the wild woman, feathered and flying as our claws and talons retract and return, tails and wings vibrant in eclectic movements. We hear her howling as one inside fire and wind, moving as nature compels her outside of logic or thought, possessed by nothing but the dance. Broken free from the conflicts of self-assessment she runs and climbs, swinging free through the wilderness of her spirit. Gnashing and thrashing and twisting and morphing in and out of our bodies is the deep instinctual call of the moment. The wild animals that live caged within our civilized barriers are freed to rove the wilderness of woman in this spirited dance!

37. A ship tips over and through jellyfish people survive to shore

Our trusted vessel has overturned and we are caught by surprise. What was steadily afloat has capsized and we are thrown into a stinging sea where survival is our sudden focus. The swim towards shore feels surreal and dreamy, the delicate jellyfish waving their poisonous pleas as they wait for us to brush by. The gentle lure of their glowing translucence seduces us with its undulation of pulse with the water, a connection to the deep slow sonar of oceanic waves. In this provocative stretch to shore, we face the strange comfort of death's peace lurking with an eerie offer of comfortable surrender. The potential pains and fatalities disguised in the fragile beauty of these wistful creatures present to us our challenge. We must avoid sinking in the way of our defeated ship and press on, because we ourselves are destined to survive.

38. Laughing people paint themselves in mud

The pure spirit of carefree play is in full demonstration. The wet earthen matter as conglomerate of local organic life is enlivened with human interaction. In our muddy hand we hold the vital energy of weather and pieces of trees that cross lifespans as well as parts of animals that have been shed or fallen away. The life of nature through time as the history of earth contains a living essence that brings the natural soul home to its origin. By bathing in mud and laughter, the creative inclination of painting it onto ourselves, we tap into the unadulterated animisms of a most basic and original human joy. We coalesce with natural infusions in this harmonious image that celebrates the primal simplicity of the earth-loving social humans in their truly organic light.

39. A choir sings a sick child to health

The fusion of vocal ranges in this choir reaches compassionately into the healing power of song. The participation of the group activates the frequencies of musical notes drawn from multiple octaves, widening the realms from which these powers are attained. The inspiration of voice into melodious tune carries the manifestation of spoken word into even further dimensions of supernatural spheres as music. The combination of word and song invokes a doubly divine access through the intentions of the lyrics and the mysterious effects musical pitches and rhythms have on our beings, the force here strong enough indeed to heal the sick child. The healing measures exemplified in this devoted singing affirms our faith in the power of music as medicine. With this faithful dispensation we are retuned to a healthy balance remaining grateful for the remedy of song eternally available for invocation to heal the tender and sick.

40. An old man recovers his heart with a buried treasure box he found

An old man finds a buried treasure box that contains enough power to recover his heart. Something archaic is aching to be unearthed to free us from a hardened heart and since it is hidden, it will take work to uncover this recuperative box. We must chip away at the rough dirt that has petrified our emotional well-being, and dig into that which it conceals. There is an old vestige of meaning or memory that is asking to be shaken clean and restored into a warm and heartful feeling. We are led into the fields to investigate what lies

46

heavy underground and axe away at calcifications that have enclosed our hearts and made them colder. We have an important mission to release resentment and soften the scabs of old wounds, recalibrating our reminiscences from a place of redemption that rekindles our spirit and capacity to love. As the man is old, we are reminded that it is never too late to set forth with a lively heart into new terrain where fresh treasures await our discovery.

41. Rattles and maracas draw spirits to a bonfire

A ceremony of spirit crackles in the fiery snaps of this energetic night where bodies left behind can travel formless on winds of song. Shapes of the rhythms drawn by claws and bones, shards of living things rattled in shells, conjure spirits to attend this festive fire. Rattles and maracas sound of sands and salts, inviting us to move through time in this wild percussion, our spirits combusted and dancing as fire, souls slipped from our spines. Freed from our barrier of skin, we flow with the fluid music of earth's pebbled rumble shaking out a beat from the ether as it banters with the flame. Leaping around the blaze in transient flashes of light, the portals are open to the spirit realm where its forces become the magnetism that draws us deeper into the fire.

42. Lightning strikes and a world leader is born

A descent of sudden illumination hammers down from the sky. A strike of immensity has realized the birth of a world leader. This propitious moment is the heavenly signature of a new age ahead, and though the leader is just born, it is now we begin the worldly preparation. The high voltage of this initial spark delivers a charge strong enough to carry this powerful current all the way to its promise. However, as for now we've only the catalyst and the desirability of the result is undetermined, it is wise to note any affect we may have on switching the transistors on and off as this influence matures into its great significance. The impulse of this electrified seed has a special momentum of great potential that must remain energized and faithfully nurtured to deliver an optimistic result.

43. An owl makes a nest for his young

The owl's wings reach deep into the night, spanning worlds of darkness from wisdom to death. Here is the nesting process, a cradle of contents collected to support the development of new eyes soon ready to peer into midnight's world. Preparing to lay the visions of the night as knowledge of the owl who sees what we do not as we are sleeping, nocturnal sights are spawning. Watching over the world of darkness, this great bird knows what we cannot, its stone cold eyes at home in the hours of the departed. The message of the owl communicates a secret knowing forbidden to us in the waking world, and thus this visitation compels us to search beyond the daylit perception of sight to reveal a deeper meaning that has yet to hatch. This baby owl is born where it belongs, in the dark home of its natural nest, where fresh eyes will soon begin a new journey into the realms of night and wisdom yet unseen.

44. The strongest people racing through wheat fields

This image throws us into the center of competitive action. The strongest people are at the height of their game in this race through wheat fields, which may be a victorious display of rich agriculture made fertile by their tending, or perhaps it is more serious as a struggle for survival. There is an endurance required in this sprint through the fields, and whether by sport or necessity, our speed and stamina are put to the test. We are called to rise to the occasion with a sense of determination, ready to run in earnest to the finish. The more durable and ready we are to face this challenge, the greater the providence as we demonstrate our best in accord with the productive fields full of strong people. Regardless of our placement in the race, we are swept into its exhilaration where, if we are willing to step our feet onto the path and go for it, exaltations of self-worth and confidence are waiting to be kicked up in the fields, likely showing us we are capable of much more than we thought.

45. Two enemies make peace as they together watch the birth of a fawn

A rivalry has been demolished at this miraculous display of nature. Something so rare and precious as witnessing the wild birth of a fawn has tamed the hatred between two enemies. As they share this gifted encounter, they are struck with a humility that inspires forgiveness and peace. They have a sudden capacity to remove the illusions of arrogant enemy-hood and to realize the uselessness of their resentments. Entrusted with this spontaneous gift of wild birth, we are cleared for a fresh look at what discords we may forgive or forget. The gracious doe and her baby have compelled us to release our grudges and turn our focus instead towards the ways of wonder and tend to the experiences that bond us.

46. A beautiful woman perfects her self portrait

The full bloom of a woman's confidence is celebrated in this artistic victory. With the self-portrait described as perfect, this devoted practice has taken time and effort. This satisfying rendition of her own image exhibits a dual understanding, first from a reflective spirit, how she sees and feels herself to appear, and second, how her physical form is presented to the outside world. This is a woman's journey of finding genuine confidence and self-love while simultaneously working to earn it by developing her artistic skill, and taking a good hard honest look at herself while she is at it. We become fully beautiful when we shine with the sheen of self-acceptance, an authentic radiance that exudes a true undeniable beauty. With this, our best possible selves are able to unfold and expand into fuller and deeper expression, as we further refine our skills and arts. When we build and sustain our self-worth by continually improving ourselves, then like the woman, we are able to elaborate this poise and extend it into everything we do.

47. A man pounds leather for his family to make clothes

This family demonstrates domestic hard work and cooperation as they share the task of making clothes. The man is establishing a steady preparatory foundation for his family to cut and sew homemade leather garments, a material sure to be durable and long lasting. The sturdiness of their occupation shows a self-reliance and capacity to generate value for income or trade. This synergy fuels a household satisfaction, supporting the family morale and productivity while validating their ability to provide for themselves. A sense of togetherness is the key of this humble collaboration. When we can work effectively with our relations and those around us, the habit of teamwork will identify and secure our own strengths. With practice, the roles and talents of each individual can be better implemented into more complex tasks, elevating the happiness and increasing the effectiveness of any group.

48. An heirloom garden is planted in rich soil

Heirloom plants have been thoughtfully tended for generations to preserve the qualities by which they were first found most favorable. The most dependable and delicious gardens are best grown from a diverse selection of heirloom seeds planted in rich soil. Since we are receiving the benefit of the conserved heirloom, we have a responsibility to maintain the purity of these distinguished seeds to keep our produce varied and diverse rather than losing the history of what was treasured and known to hybridization, which soon makes the intact species irretrievable. We have a duty to replenish the soil in this rich garden as it provides for us, planting the future with at least as much love and care as we received it. In this way we might hope to enrich all that passes through us and on to our descendants, keeping what we most love alive in our lineages and environments.

49. A mystic woman bewitches a muggle

A muggle's narrowmindedness has been broken open by the bewitchment of a mystic woman. A new world of perception is unlocked, a rigidity of thought loosened into a deeper sense of knowing. A woman with supernatural wisdom has influenced another's perspective, freeing a stubborn mind to roam the boundless worlds of magical thought. This mystical illumination ignites the imagination and creates a sense of wonder and awe in the ponderable unknowns. Living in an enchanted light allows us to navigate the unexplainable, where we may explore the vast pools of miraculous content as a gateway to broader understanding. It is a good time to be receptive to mystic influences and pay attention to our subtle perceptions to reveal messages from beyond what reaches our immediate senses.

50. An instant deluge quells a wildfire

An overwhelming force of fire needs an overwhelming force of water to restore balance in this full bodied warring of the elements. A natural equilibrium was aggressively thrown off course and required a dramatic counterweight to realign. This instant deluge came hard and fast, obliterating the hostile wildfire with a match of strength. The torrent alone may have toppled the neutral balance the opposite direction, but with the pull disruptively upset from center first by the devastating fire, the rush of water serves as a truce for the rampage of nature's dueling elements. On this monumental scale of nature's grandest storms, we juxtapose our personal imbalances to see what energetic properties we must implement to conquer mayhem and prevent catastrophes from causing undue destruction in our own lives.

51. A woman blows pollen from her hand and it flies miles

A woman's breath carries pollen for miles, impregnating the distant winds, filling the empty air with new life. This far-reaching fertile burst will distribute all the pollen holds, spreading its regenerative potential into broader lands. Already infused with the woman's breath, the essence of her spirit and intentions will affect how the pollen rides these winds and where it lands to disseminate. The mercurial aspect of such extensive mobility shows abundance and widespread influence from whatever is birthed into the atmosphere at this moment. Anything set into motion at this time will likely travel far and wide, so it is wise to note the contents and spirits of what we are breathing into life and the direction we face as we disperse them.

52. The eldest buck escapes his shooter

The eldest buck has long survived the throes of the hunted already, and here he does it again. A full rack of antlers is a coveted prize of trophy hunters, so this is an exceptionally proficient escape. A test of age proves this buck has remained strong and alert after many vulnerable years in these wild hunting grounds, his long survival a testament to his dominance. A jolt of adrenaline sharpens the nerves and refreshes one's outlook after a near-death confrontation, so the successful fleeing of this elder buck has affirmed his continued ability to endure the threats of his exposed existence. The buck reminds us that we need not wallow in fear, but we must stand strong and clear-headed to avoid falling prey to our susceptibilities. Ongoing vigilance in both body and mind will prepare us to thrive in the later stages of life as we find strength in our challenges and wake each day with gratitude for life.

53. A young class of children is taught timeless wisdom

A number of children are soaking up timeless wisdom in this hopeful promise for the future. The infusion of perennial knowledge into this impressionable group secures another round of life for these important teachings. Sometimes traditions pivotal to the advancement of the human spirit become over aggrandized or diluted and the core of their original meanings become lost. Thankfully here the authentic fundamentals have been preserved for these students to inherit, and fortunate to receive such profound wisdom directly, they now have a responsibility to carry it into their own lives and then pass it on intact with the original concepts of what made it valuable in the first place.

54. An old sick tree surprisingly bears the finest fruit later

This tree encourages us to hold faith in what appears old or sick. It is not time to let go. There is an internal vivacity churning beneath the illusory frailty that obscures whatever we are examining, the tree's true nature is alive and well. We must look deeper, as the real verve is concealed beneath the bark. Despite its sickly appearance, a well of strength remains inside, gestating new life as it prepares to produce a succulent harvest. If we believe in this old tree, if we nurture it and notice it, offer it patience and care, we will witness its revival, and along with the sweet reward of the love we have this opportunity to give, we shall later receive the gift of its finest fruit.

55. Snakes burrow into the sand to save their energy

Snakes are slick and efficient generators of power and form, ever ready to assert proactive energy and strike out to claim what they wish. As they stop to burrow into the warm sands of the quiet darkness, they begin to recharge, receiving the regenerative powers of the stable receptive earth. Productivity and exertion must pause for the silent restorative space of deep rest. In this gap between activities we conserve our resources and replenish our energy reserves so that we may return with the power of our full potential. This is a time to dream and receive inspiration within the quiet comfort of total stillness. When the snakes later reemerge, their vital energy will be settled and refocused, and maximum potencies will be ready to direct the way of decisive action once again.

56. A woman's heartbeat becomes one with a cat's purr

The complex pulses that beat and throb inside of us orchestrate our body's most intimate pressures and paces, the revelators and creators of our moods and deepest aspects of being. When these divine rhythms are synchronized between two beings, a powerfully emotional loving bond is established. The fusion of this woman's heartbeat with the mysterious purr of her beloved cat exemplifies the deep wild union only possible with an animal. As her heart is synchronized with the harmony of her blissful feline, they fuse together into a shared unit of time, a coordination that encapsulates them into a mutual wave of transcendent love that reaches far beyond words. This pulsing vibrancy is a deep soul connection of profound peace between woman and cat, human and animal, where primal feelings of love are deeply experienced in the silent language of two beating hearts that share together a single purr.

57. In an ecstatic moment a rainbow appears in the sky

Ecstasy of great heights, a rainbow in the sky! The display of colors arched over the atmosphere enamors this elated moment. As joy spreads over us and inside of us, our pleasure is aligned with this phenomenon of water and light, the heavens grant us a blessing in this shower of colorful bliss. We are in tune with the skies and supported with grace from above. In the light of celebration, we impress this timely rainbow into the inner linings of our souls, and allow this full spectrum to bathe us in its radiance. When our own highest delights are syncopated with the moment a rainbow spreads over the sky, we receive an affirmation that we are in accord with the harmonies of the universe in our present hopes and desires.

58. A tribal woman carves into a boulder

Carving into a boulder is a gesture of permanence. Whether this woman is etching freely or inscribing something specific, knowledge will be later derived from this present exposition. A foundation is laid that will instruct the future, the knowledge in this symbol will be taught to others and pondered upon. Etched in stone, its message will be long lasting and interpreted throughout spans of time between which they are forgotten and then rediscovered again. Inside this far reaching line of awareness we contemplate the ways we inform and guide other human wanderers as they pass along and read what we have marked. It is a chance to chisel a signpost of our most thoughtful choosing into something that resembles the strata of forever.

59. A curious child unwinds a spool of thread and rewinds it

In a mode of curiosity and discovery we are prepared to learn, and the first solution will not satisfy. We must attempt our endeavor with the playful wonder of a child and the tenacity and patience of an inquisitive mind. If we approach all things with a fresh spirit of interested engagement, a lively curiosity, we can appreciate the infinite details of possibility in everything we do. We can see the amazing fact that no matter how many times the child winds and unwinds the spool of thread, it will never twice be done in exactly the same way. Every time, every effort, is a new rendition completely unique from the next. We strive to maintain our childlike wonder as adults so that persistent innovation and openness will prevent boredom, stagnation, or conceit while promoting a strong and agile mind that supports lifelong learning and growth.

60. A man with a sword guides another man into the light

The man with the sword, already initiated in the ways of his weapon, guides the other into this special knowing, leading him to the light that shines from the blade. There is a responsibility bestowed from the dominant man to his acolyte, an archetype of manhood passed down to one worthy of receiving this transmission. The way of the sword as a martial path gives respectful power to the natural warrior, a discipline that requires dedication and training, traditional forms kept intact. Bringing his disciple into the light, the man with the sword shares the virility of his weapon with highest regard to the fighting art, aware that such sacred knowledge systems should be bequeathed only to those who will honor the respected teachings of the weapon. The way of the sword teaches a fierce poise, a controlled stamina contained in its sheath, resting but ready to strike if darkness attacks that which the warrior inside of us protects as the light.

61. A crunch of dry leaves is the only sound under animal's feet

There is an invisible presence alone here with only an animal and the small crunches its feet make over the leaves. There is no one else. It is eerie, quiet, dry, and still. We are suspended by a strange absence, pausing from the sounds and conversation that keep society turning. We witness quiet nature as it stands without observation, this moment a hiatus from human life, we ourselves hovering and ghostlike. The atmosphere is so tranquil that the wild hum of anticipation is buzzing at the edge of its arrival. A silent calmness asks us to stop and wait, to observe the subtleties that only the wilderness knows. When this remote quiet effectively shows us how to listen, with what we hear we may trek forth again with a deeper connection to the wisdom of silence along with a finer attunement to the vast wilderness ever ahead of our step.

62. Laughing people trade jobs for the day and it goes well

There are joyful people working amongst each other who decide to switch jobs for the day. A routine is broken in this good humored rotation, and it goes well. The individuals themselves are confident enough to assert their efforts to the challenges of unfamiliar tasks. The presence of laughter intercepts the possible intrusive fear of the unknown, and all carry on lightheartedly. The obligation of honest work circulates through the workplace as they trust one another with each other's duties. We know the day turns out well, so we are prompted to try out an unordinary approach to our own day. Spontaneity supersedes predictability in this interlude, a reprieve from our regular work. With laughter as our companion, we sidestep our usual perspective today and have fun trading roles with those around us.

63. A book burner is tossed into the fire and reborn

This brash succession of fiery annihilation has induced a quick cycle of death and rebirth. In this tight interval, the book burner has been burned and then born into a new life, a complete turning over of the self in a short time span. An inferno sweeps by in a sweltering flash where we are new again, a lifetime away from both what we ourselves have destroyed and also what has destroyed us, which as we now see are one and the same. The blazes of our own undoing have crumbled to ash and may be finally forgotten. Whether or not we are forgiven, however, will be determined by what we throw into the next round of flames when the fire comes again.

64. A secret Buddha sheds his grace anonymously

Generosity without pride is its purest form, the composure of grace in this picture. The honest pleasure of giving as its own reward is kept clean by anonymity, ensuring the recipient that there is no need for recognition and no debt of any kind is due. The giver's secret known only by the omniscience of holy eyes enlivens a faith in the recipient as well as the heart of the benefactor, as a true goodness is tangible in these deepest motivations that ideally direct all of our thoughts and actions. This Buddha inspires us towards kindness not for credit or praise or to appear goodhearted to others, but for its own sake and the happiness we feel inside our own hearts. Implementing this compassionate anonymous generosity into the smallest actions of our daily gestures becomes the collection of moments that build our days, and then our lives. The most precious generosity lives as an authentic hub of private space only we secretly know, the impulse of unspoken kindness behind everything we think and do.

65. A woman makes jewelry to decorate the goddess

This is a presentation from woman to goddess, a communion of the divine feminine. By honoring the goddess as distinct from ourselves, we worship her as the world mother, from where we came and to whom we desire to return, the source of all life and longing. As the woman dedicates her time and energy to making this jewelry she exalts the goddess within herself as creator, the beauty of her highest spirit. This moment calls to ornament the goddess with an artistic creation made by our own hands, to honor her within or through our lover, through our sisters and mothers, unto all aspects of the feminine principles we cherish. We praise the universal female energy, admiring her in the realms of spirit and our everyday lives, today with a sacred adornment offered by the inspired efforts of our own creation.

66. Under an enchanted tree and aromatic roses lovers kiss

Magic has its hold in this dreamscape of lovers. The tree is enchanted, an enraptured paradise envelops us in the shimmer of its warm glow. Fragrant with roses, the silken petals slip the scent of romance and desire into the space. Aromatic oils release a steamy river of passion into the stream of lovers. Sparks are flying and love is alive as they kiss beneath mystical witness. This setting encourages the lovers' deep connection, nature's support on full multisensorial display. The thirst of longing is soaked with joy in this picturesque delight of sensual infusion. Absorbed in romantic bliss we lock lips with our lover, the beauty they hold as the loveliest rose, this enchanted kiss, our highest delight.

67. People are shivering and then brought freshly cut wool

People here are at the mercy of the cold, presumably dramatic as its amelioration is by wool. Thankfully the discomfort is short lived, since within the snapshot of this picture fresh wool is cut and distributed. This informs us that a compassionate process is underway to liberate us from our present suffering. On the other side of this uneasy chill, there is sturdy warm relief, but for now, we must survive by the warmth of our own breath until the grace of salvation arrives. We become stronger if we acknowledge our challenge while affirming our willingness to endure the difficulty. It is sensible to notice our needs, particularly where we are self-sufficient and for what we rely upon others to provide, and consider if we need to rearrange our dependencies. At the same time it is crucial to understand that we all need support from others in various ways, and it is imperative we maintain the capacity to graciously receive without shame or guilt. Everyone needs help sometimes!

68. Two dolphins hop the setting sun on the horizon

This is a sublime occasion where multiple factors are aligned to create this idyllic moment. From the serenity of the shore we gaze along the shimmering waters into the distant orange sky where dolphins draw this fleeting arc over the setting sun. There is a prominent indication that we are in the right place at the right time, as our exact perspective is what creates the illusion of the dolphins' leap over the sun-capped horizon. We are in a fortunate location to witness something rare, a convergence of beautiful wonders overlayed in perfect framing. The unique chance of this visual gift calls us into the wake of beauty to seek an extraordinary vision heightened beyond usual experience.

69. Two squirrels quarrel for nuts but then end up sharing

A competitive quarrel occurs between two like beings, each asserting their power to prove domination over the other. With the common goal of procuring an ample food stash, they clash at first as they fight for the entire supply. In a mysterious change of heart they end up sharing, leading us to contemplate why. Perhaps they realized their likeness and understood in fairness that there was enough to satisfy them both. Maybe they saw more would be lost in a continued battle, the risk of injury or the inevitable exhaustion after a rancorous quarrel. Yes, if we seek we find, and if we work for something we earn it, but we must not over consume, especially at the expense of another's total loss. These two squirrels show us the way to reconciliation as we are asked to avoid excessive greed for the wider benefit of our common kind.

70. A girl is saved by a bear attack by befriending it

A girl is spared from a bear attack, thwarting its threatening approach by befriending the beast. Just as the girl sacrifices nothing of herself to the bear, we avoid mistaking foolish naivete for friendship and must continue to defeat our fears by allowing no part of ourselves to fall prey. Instead we interact with our perceived enemy in a strategic manner, appearing invulnerable with our confident attitude. In this spirit, we demonstrate our courage by assuming that fear will not overthrow us and therefore we will not be taken by it. Rather than falling afraid, we do not entertain the idea of attack in the first place, which strips us of the tantalizing fear so savory to our attacker. Beyond this, a further revelation is possible that the bear never intended attack, and that the shadow of fright was of our own making.

71. Books of myths scattered on tables

A vast study is spread out and calls us to read these books, easily accessible and ready to open. Exposure to mythologies and old stories allows us to explore ourselves by noticing how we respond to the tales of others outside of our own situation. Myths are gems that have been filtered through time, archives of archetypal human events, compulsions, and tendencies common to all people. Within this quest for knowledge we find a deep rooted sense of our humanity and gain insight beyond our present culture and our own ego. We travel into the stories where we relate to our likenesses and feel our aversions as we compare and contrast ourselves in this journey through the archetypes. Reading myth reveals our true nature, what we love, what infuriates us, and everything in between.

72. A long time splinter is removed

A splinter is a small but mighty invasion that brings substantial pain, especially in this case, having been embedded deep into the skin as evident by its lengthy assault. But finally, the long term annoyance is eradicated. The jab of this wooden prick is pulled from our skin and we are relieved of our irritation at last. The intrusion of the tiny shard exits without a trace, allowing us to move forward unscarred. In all misfortunes, large and small, there is a lesson to be learned, and excised with the splinter itself we also remove the likelihood of its return, ensuring that in the future it will not so easily enter us again. With a breath of fresh air we are freed from this nuisance once and for all, comfortable and in pain no more.

73. A woman sits in lotus by a creek

This is a scene of tranquil yet conscious meditation, the fresh water in the flowing creek one of the most opulent sources of serene energy. There is a steady composure in the woman's balance, her engaged relaxation stabilized by the earth's hold, invigorated by the flow of the singing sinuous waters. Sitting in lotus is the posture of the yogi, so this is not a casual calm state, but a focused one that is transcendent and deep. In stillness we let go into the soft fluid rush of the stream. As we merge with the rippling waters, the silence of our own presence becomes the vital restoration that strengthens our health and connection to source, the peaceful lull of meditation in nature.

74. An imaginary mermaid saves a believing child

Imagination is our saving grace, something that benefits us throughout our entire lives. Without the conditioning of what we are taught and our own accumulation of experiences, we, like the child, are able to see things in a more original and imaginative light. We are able to feel into the creation of our own images as the mermaid is conjured here and use them for our own aid and comfort. The freedom of our imagination allows us to cast a line into the vivid pool of our own subconscious where we swim through our heroes and dreams, our questions and answers, the inclinations that seem to ever bubble up to the surface, giving us insight to what needs addressed in our individually unique worlds. Seeing the mermaid, we intuit a watery emotional aspect to our current healing, the medicine already dwelling in our own lagoons of deep waters, where from within ourselves, the savior is brought to life.

75. Millions of flowers blossom at once all over the world

A widespread renaissance of enormous proportion is birthed. These fresh florals are the pinnacle of beauty in this great time of achievement and bounty unfolding. This is the beginning of a climactic increase, the lush blossoms promising ample fruits still to come. Millions flowering so exuberantly together is a positive symbiotic indication of an entire magnitude of being, complete and far-reaching. This is a time of renewal, ensuring peace and prosperity as we approach the peak of this golden age. We enjoy this vast display of beauty, an auspicious time to celebrate and connect with others, mutually uplifted by the great fragrance of this massive bloom.

76. Precious metals have value and meaning

There are many metals abundant in the earth's mantle, but precious metals are limited and rare. Here we are asked to look at what is precious in our lives and show appreciation for those special things we possess or experience. Not only do these geological elements contain practical value but many are also esteemed for their energetic potency and symbolic meaning. In an applied sense we recognize resources are limited so we should optimize use of rare materials and distribute their worth as currency respectfully and wisely. Likewise, precious artifacts and people in our lives should be appreciated and honored, cared for and maintained, preserved as special in every way possible. Take nothing for granted!

77. Glass breaks but it is remade into something more beautiful

Broken glass is irksome, leaving jagged pieces and sharp edges that can cut us. Something has crashed down and we must pick it up, accepting that it is no longer what it was. It is for us to make it more beautiful now, situations and objects alike. We are asked to see the fragments in the full light of their fractures and begin to rearrange them. Whatever material we are dealing with has cracked or shattered giving us the opportunity to resurrect the pieces and shape them into a renewed aesthetic. Optimism is critical here because a proactive choice must be made to actually clean up the mess and then make the most of its components. As we gather the parts, a more beautiful whole will take form as the cohesion of the caring spirit behind this improvement is fabricated into the outcome.

78. Rocky mountains host a religious pilgrimage

Rocky mountains indicate tough terrain, so this is a pilgrimage of intense dedication. We are called to embark on a challenging journey to explore and enhance our spiritual life. The path ahead compels us to connect with our holiest callings and oblige them with our commitment. We rise to the occasion of paying homage to our divine center, whether it is a physical pilgrimage or one of the heart expressed through meditation or study. We demonstrate to the highest consciousnesses that live within and outside of our bodies that we are neither lazy nor weak, and that we have gratitude for our lives and all we are given. Ready to step onto this rigorous road, the first inquiry is our proposed destination and also to whom or what we are devoted. This long open trail ahead asks us to search for the spiritual affinities latent in ourselves that long to serve a higher power. A journey that takes time and courage is forthcoming, and though the expedition may not be easy, the certainty of a new strength and understanding waits at the finish, the place of our eternal longing.

79. A group of lepers chant their way to recovery

Chants are specific vibrations of vowel-based frequencies that transpose the realm of sound to affect physical realities. When practiced with intention and focus they are conduits of great power, their potencies increasing as more resonances join their cumulative wavelengths. Certain mantras have retained and gained significance over time, developing tremendous aptitude for healing and facilitating change, a universal timbre that those in tune with their harmony may tap into. Voice bends the waves of air and light around us, and as the lepers show us in this dramatic miraculous recovery, it truly is the force that sculpts the form. Our present chant produces the intended effects, so without spending too much time wondering how or why, we experiment with intentional mantras to see if we can cure our most serious ailments.

80. A woman who wove her own robe can escape through thorns

This is a hearty and capable woman who is prepared to execute her own escape. She has the skill and perseverance to make her own way, even if she must pass this thorny barrier. Assured by her own self-reliance, having already woven her protective guard, she is ready to prevail against any tumultuous circumstance by the efforts of her own doing. Dressed in the sturdy shield of her own sewn garment, this independent woman teaches us a route to autonomy by claiming victory over tremulous forebodings with a self-derived strength to escape that which entraps us. We have the fortitude to brandish our shields as necessary, and map our own paths to self-chosen freedoms. Only we truly know what constitutes our individual liberty, and we will never know our full strengths and skills until we put them to the test.

81. Roots of giant trees cool hot feet in the desert

Foundations joined, these giant trees support our mission, the solace of their big shade and wide sprawling roots give us a break to cool our hot desert feet. Depending on how many hours or miles we have endured this discomfort, we could be recuperating from quite a grueling journey, barefoot and burned on the hot dry sand. This shady refuge soothes us and connects us with the groundwork of all nature, roots to feet, fully supported and welcomed in this abode of giant trees where we are substantial ourselves in their mighty shadow. It is important to prevent overheating and exhaustion by relaxing in the refreshing comfortable coolness of these magnificent trees, our roots intertwined, as our soles absorb the blessing of this reprieve.

82. A woman hums to charm a snake

We see a woman in her mystical reverie humming to enchant this snake. The allure of her hum pulls the serpent into this wordless song as we imagine them gyrate in sync with each other's stare, linking them into this same wave of being. In this shared trance, they dance along subtle cusps of energy in the hypnotics of the charm. The snake embodies our deepest instincts and drives, where strikes are coiled and uncoiled, subdued and thrust. The woman's delicate penetration into this energy field using the medium of her mesmerizing hum protects her from snakebite and shows her ability to tame dragons while receiving the raw power the snake offers in this exchange.

83. Shields and arrows fight off invaders

A present invasion has us on defense, and fortunately we are
equipped to fight. As with any attack, we must be aware of the
perpetrators and what they intend so that we know how to respond.
In times of battle, whether we are combating an illness in our body or
intruders at home, or even a mental distraction as a psychic assault,
we must first and foremost attempt clear-mindedness. If our senses
are sharp we have the acuity to decisively execute with a speedy mind,
and when we balance this with ability to calculate the right move with
fierce competence, we find the fulcrum of strategy that will win our
battles. Aligned with the truest good in ourselves we face the
invaders, unafraid to call upon the warrior inside, shields and arrows
ready.

84. A girl passes into womanhood fanned by feathers

This is an honored maturation of a girl becoming a woman, the
spirit of sanctity rides the wind as she is fanned by feathers. The
celebration feels tribal and pure, a coming of age that has earned this
ritualistic respect. An entire change of self is imminent in this major
life transition, new responsibilities and privileges ready to transform
the girl's whole world as she steps into a completely different societal
role. The waving wings send a breeze of supportive encouragement
into the air of this new flight. This is a time to rise up and onward
from a childish phase, letting a part of us shed away as we move
forward from the past. We are elevating into a space of clarity and
open potential, a fresh beginning. This ceremony affirms that the
new woman contains the womb of life, and like her, we are prepared

to gestate and birth whatever we choose to accept into our own fertile vessel of creation and life.

85. A giant tortoise peeks from his shell for the first time in years

This giant tortoise has been in a state of slumber, sedated by some willful hibernation or debilitation for many years, tucked inside of his shell with no external perception or experience. Though so far only a peek, a curious wakefulness emerges as he abandons this long inertia. Having closed off sight from the sun and all other life, an initial glimpse of hope is cast in this new light, a necessary motivational change for any living being. There is an intimation of a growing openness along with a broadened view of life beyond one's own familiar domain. The giant tortoise suggests to us by example that even if our eyelids open slowly, even if we proceed inch by inch, something else lies beyond the backs of our own eyes, beyond the roof of our own shell.

86. People work together to assemble straw huts

Assembling straw huts takes us to primitive circumstances, a group survival dependent on communal work, shared exertions for a common benefit. The abundance of straw is by itself a less than sturdy building material, but when tied together as bales or reinforced by wooden frames, or anything else conceivable within the contributions of the group mind, it is both insulate and breathable, an ideal component of a traditional hut. When people work cooperatively, much can be accomplished in a short while and with better results made possible by diverse skillsets. Building this natural shelter with our fellow humans gives us a mood of productivity and cooperation. We will be soon sheltered in the warmth of comfort and safety after the collective achievement shared with our closest people.

87. Screaming hollers of victory through night insects

The orchestra of night is alive with crickets, cicadas, and other singers of the humid dark. This is a song praising lush dampness, wet life soaked with sustenance and reproductive possibility. A healthy insect population promotes a vigorous ecosystem, making clear that this environment is booming with life and abundance. The interdependence of life from insect to plant to bird to grazers to predators and everything in between is boosted by these bugs screaming their victorious hollers. This robust insect population signifies a locally existential swing towards equilibrium, reminding us of our human responsibility to protect the wildlands around us, respecting these essential critters not as pests, but as something imperative to the wellbeing of all species on earth. A harmonious dreamscape of life is audible tonight.

88. An egg inside an egg inside an egg

This trifecta shows three generations of females as a maternal continuity, a succession of daughters, each egg contained within the next. It is interesting to note that a woman already holds her entire life supply of eggs at birth, so that as long as a lineage of women lives on, this sense of perpetual existence continues as an egg within an egg within an egg. We can contemplate our partial selves, half of our biologically potential lives existing as unfertilized eggs within our own mothers at her birth, and she within our maternal grandmothers onto our great-grandmothers and so on, all the way back to the matrilineal source of our genealogical beginnings. As budding blossoms born from mother flowers, secret vessels kept sealed from womb to womb, we hold motherhood sacred. This is a profound realization that awakens the mysterious relationship to our long intricate lineage of many mothers.

89. A bare foot grasps around a stone

The articulation of a bare foot grasping a stone establishes an immediate intimacy between human and nature. Direct contact from skin to stone absorbs the pure life force of this mineral composite, a transmitter of earth's vital energy. Furthermore, the sole of the foot is one of the most penetrable openings into the body's energy channels, so this link makes our bond to earth substantial. By flexing the toes around the stone, we exert more of our own effort into the energetic threshold of this connection, maximizing the energy flow transmitted, our systems fully engaged. This rooted dexterity marks our calling to the stones and boulders where we are ready to leap sure-footed into the wild path that calls us forth.

90. Spoonfuls of dark brown honey are the cure

Dark brown honey, the raw essence of the local land concocted by the magic of bees, offers by the spoonful its powerful cure. Among the purest and most original of all natural medicines, honey is the nectar that carries the symbiotic fluid of life that stimulates and sustains all species in a given environment. In the divine exchange of pollination and food production between flowers and bees, the subtle ingredients of the anticipated honey run like plasma through the ecosystem's veins collecting enzymes and nutrients along the way, building natural defenses against pathogens and allergens, ultimately creating a perfectly tailored curative potion. The delicious pleasure of this sweet holistic medicine is an adaptogen, harmonizing the conditions of our own bodies with the environment around us, a foundational principle of health and wellness. The apothecary is open, our cure is boldly stated in this message of natural remedy.

91. A scorpion slides under a drummer's hand unnoticed

An undetected threat is sliding under the immediate space of the drummer's hand, into the zone of its rhythmic touch. The beat of the percussion determines whether we slap down onto an inevitable reactionary sting or instead happen to raise our hand in concurrence with the scorpion's passing. It seems possible that the musician was so enraptured with the drum that the creative trance was protective, a positive distraction from fear that prevented any disturbance from the passing scorpion. This visitation reminds us to trust the music, to dissolve into our most honest rhythms and stay on pace as this possible sting is lurking, a poison of the underworld slipping by unnoticed. In the image the precarious arachnid passes along overlooked, the timing works in the drummer's favor, the song as it plays shall continue, and as long we don't alter the natural beat, our current pacing is right on mark.

92. A parade of animals crosses bridges and gates at night

Animals use the cloak of night to travel new domains, protected in the dark, hidden from human eyes. In the privacy of their nocturnal world, they cross bridges and gates to search for food or shelter, claiming new territory as they scavenge and hunt for possibility. A parade of animals at first seems ridiculous, yet it illustrates how little humans really know of the secret communications and behaviors of animals as they exist when we are not looking. This parade could represent the pageant of our own animalistic selves voyaging into the night, across our everyday bridges and through our usual gates, exploring beyond normal thresholds of consciousness. As morning comes, we might laugh at this march of the animals and begin the day happy, or perhaps a sense of rewilding will have opened new frontiers for our psyches to roam, transcending the limitations of our normal daytime waking state dominated by human logic and thought.

93. Natural confetti of falling leaves drops in celebration

The season is shifting in this autumnal celebration, a growth cycle has completed and the tree turns skeletal again, stripping away what is old to receive new life. What no longer serves the process of growth has fallen dry, and with such festive sights as confetti falling as leaves, our outlook is certainly positive during this transition. The old leaves have fulfilled their purpose for the growth and life of the tree, and as we celebrate this colorful change of cycle, there is a beautiful acceptance in the revolutions of time, inevitable changes of scenery made lovely. This is not a party for artificial manmade decorations, but an event that calls for creative imagination using the provided material of the natural world to rejoice in this turning of time.

94. Women paint each other's faces in the moonlight

The moonlight reflects the sun's light as these women reflect each other. Through this shared play, the women interpret and validate one another as they pull their inner souls to the surface with paint, recognizing and artistically interpreting their unique characteristics, distinguishing the spirit of each woman from the collective group. When we feel seen and understood by others we are fortified, we step into our holistic role, we integrate our elements of character and our selfhood expands. Facepainting brings to life the wild spirit within, objective appearance heeds to the invisible self that longs to be seen. Partially concealed under this graceful moonlight, we gather a group of women or friends to mutually support one another's deep soul expression in this creative play.

95. A warm morning breakfast at a cold icy farm

A cold icy farm in the morning makes our bones feel rigid and tight. We don't want to move, yet we are offered a fresh cooked breakfast as a warm invitation into the day. With the uncertainty of food as a reality on a winter farm, this satiation comforts us deep inside, warming up our digestive juices and pumping our blood with fresh nutrition and energy. Fueled for the day, we count every single meal as a small victory in a time that could easily leave us rationing food with limited supply. Fed on the farm we are nourished, energized and ready to complete our duties as we warm ourselves and prepare the land to sustain future crops, looking forward to the fertile spring. As the farm feeds us, we too must feed the farm. May every bite be precious.

96. Thunder shakes broken musical instruments back to life

Music's mystery lives as close to gods as anything, sacred math that evades logical explanation in the harmonies and relationships of its scales and measures. As the sonic houses of music, instruments are the sources of soul stimulation and movement in a way nothing else comes close. Broken instruments revived by the command of thunder is a musical awakening inseminated by divine power, a booming proclamation that strikes heavy with inspiration ready to unleash. A tune is shaking in the atmosphere demanding it be born, a force larger than life is on the verge of breaking into profound music. Our human touch is necessary to give structure to this divine burst of thunder cracking in the skies, a rumble that commands renovation of what is broken and forgotten, the song of the muse shaking our world and asking that we play it.

97. A butterfly lays its delicate legs on the thorn

The delicate legs of the butterfly land on the thorn with grace, a respectful and cautious approach to the plant that stands by protecting itself from predatory intruders. Like the butterfly, we are vulnerable in our fragility and must navigate the thorned thatches with awareness of our susceptibilities and aim for soft landings. The threat of the thorn does not dissuade the pollinator from the flower it seeks, but requires finesse to reach the stalk and find the nectar without getting punctured or trapped, a defense system the plant needs to thrive in its own right. Nature is intelligent, filled with these built-in harmonies, and if we take a moment to study such cues of welcome and warning, knowing when to approach and when to withdraw, how to quietly land without harm, we can read and interact with the nuances of our world in a similar way.

98. A long metal vessel of sacrificial herbs

Sacrificial herbs have been gathered with intention and purpose, an offering collected for the spiritual world. Metals are the ultimate energy conductors, so this large vessel promises maximum energetic transmission of the preparation inside. The herbal combination intact in the vessel is set to fulfill its mission, to connect with the spirit of the sacrifice. This is a healing prayer, a sacrificial dedication that presents the sacred to the sacred, our intent sealed up and ready for ceremonial presentation. The herbal energies wrapped up in the long metal vessel are arranged to effectively deliver the contents of our message, including all we have psychically contributed. Before sending it off we imbue one last breath of intent, never underestimating the effect of our every thought and gesture.

99. The ceiling and rug are exactly the same in a holy place

As above, so below, a timeless esoteric truth. We are hermetically sealed in this holy place, a reflected semblance between ceiling and floor, earth and sky. The floor beneath our humble human footsteps is glorified by this exalted rug, exactly the same as the ceiling above, the symbolic heaven where gods roam. A multidimensional volume expands this divine portal and gives us heavenly bearings, the macrocosm of the greater universe aligned with our individual footsteps. A divine image shines down as a mirror onto our own congregational path, our worship receiving a benediction from the holy eyes that see us in this place. The macrocosm as a larger pattern, an array containing the identical design of our microcosm, moves us to the truth that to be one with the sacred, we must enter the abode of worship and raise our earthly selves to meet the highest, where heaven and earth unite to become one and the same.

100. A spirit in the sky is actually jumping stars

Out of the barriers of time and place, the actuality of a flying star spirit is emphasized. The entity is literally jumping stars, catapulting through vast sweeps of astronomical distance, leaping over great bounds of limitless space. Without the restriction of form, this reality invites us to journey into dreamworlds far beyond our physical constraints and allow our unharnessed selves to project outside of practicality into the impossible. With this dream preceding the steps that will follow in the physical world, our potentials are much greater with this threshold of possibility cast faraway into the stars. It is a time of reaching new heights, where the unattainable may actually be realized. A rising star is calling us to chase our dreams into this grand escape where we are free to wander our wildest possibilities.

101. Clams and barnacles clipping the toxins of the sea

Clams and barnacles together siphon the sea where there is apparently plenty of detritus to filter in this active effort. We can shield these important custodians from damage if we eliminate the harmful toxins they consume as bottom feeders. If we accumulate less artificial material so that we dispose of less, mitigating plastic and chemical pollutants, we can protect our oceans and prevent a contaminated bionetwork. This way our waste products will be more natural and clean, and toxins will not leach so heavily into the great circle of life we all inhabit. A moment of thanks and recognition for the beings of land and sea, cleanup crews of all kinds, whose janitorial work serves to detoxify and clean up our world. May we all play our parts to keep the food chains clean from the bottom up for the benefit of the entire earth.

102. Dancing freely in a spinning dress at dawn

Swept into the whimsical dance of the whirling dress we slip into its airy motion, spinning our own momentums for the day. In the rotary of this free movement we send vibrations into the dawn that will determine how the rest of the day follows. If we sync our waking spirit with the mood we want to tune into, we can choreograph our daily dance with our chosen resonance from the very beginning. The twirling dress at dawn is a rhythm that sets an upbeat metronome for the day, creating a spiral of magnetism that pulls us in a positive direction, a coil through time that answers back to the day's first calls. One step leads to the next, so with the gift of lightness and freedom in this dance, may we spin the best energy we can into the freshness of each morning.

103. Bows and arrows striking marks on trees

A skilled archer exemplifies pristine vision and focus, a relaxed but determined effort. Mark after mark of success is shown as we continually hit the target. A steady one pointed concentration between self and target is required for us to repeatedly hit the mark. The aim must be linearly accurate but also aligned with the breath, the air on which the arrow rides as we release it. When we can fully envision hitting the bull's eye flight after flight, we are able to merge with the perfect moment of release, the arrow simply following through with the path of connection we made in our mind. Our strategy for success is not rash or hasty, neither aggressive nor brutish or even extroverted, but alone, quiet and meditative. We become one with the arrow as we intensely visualize the goal, an inner awareness fused with detailed observation, a patience maintained until precision has become certain.

104. The moment an injured dog knows it will be okay and walks again

This is the specific moment our difficulty changes course, a distinct transition from suffering to improvement. A tension has broken, the drag of defeat has snapped and given way to this revival. Uncertainty of recovery is a substantial part of an injury's strain, so this emotional moment gives us considerable relief. The dog walks again, finally ready to bounce back, and though we know we are coming up from behind, starting from a point of relative weakness, our ascent is certain. Whether we have held the pain in ourselves or for a loved one such as this dog, we are overjoyed with this redemptive resilience, strength reclaimed. With the right outlook, those who survive the greatest challenges and traumas often come back even stronger than before, enhanced with a depth of perspective and a newfound appreciation for their health and strength. Now with each step forward, the damage falls further and further behind. Up and onward!

105. A foolish one gets deeply lost in a cave

A foolish one has transgressed their limits. Boundaries have been overstepped and one has lost sight from where they came. Dizzy and disoriented, all sense of direction has been confused, and vanished into the darkness they are deeply unsure of the way out of the cave.

We do not know the outcome here, the lost one may become further perplexed and hopeless if they do not redirect themselves. If called into the dark cave for epochal adventure, however, the lost fool is positioned to venture boldly into the unknown, where a lack of experience accelerates growth by necessity, an act of bravery that leads some to their greatest destinies. To grow into the profound individual they are to become, the fool fit to journey must innovate under desperation and develop character through tests of hardship. Otherwise, the lost one fails and is foolish indeed. The displaced fool first needs to admit they are lost, and whether the journey is a return home or to press on through the cave no matter how arduous, they have the chance to come back as a worthy hero with the boon of experience.

106. A child walks up stairs in a public building for a life duty

This child rises to an early calling, a life duty declared. A statement of purpose at such a tender age shows an inherent propensity for this youth to work for the public. Any innate talents or passions demonstrated in the early years should be recognized as signs that help us guide the developing child towards their highest destiny. If we view ourselves as the children we once were, recalling our first tastes of authentic interest and pure joy, we can remember our own genuine natures. The recollection of our earliest hobbies and happiness, the things that felt effortless yet impelled further curiosity, the participations that were of their own reward, will help us find our way forward during any stage of life.

107. Howling wolves break a long time silence

A long silence insinuates an eeriness, a looming death or a captured spirit frozen in time, a suspenseful haunting that hovers until broken. This quiet stillness has lasted a while, a brittle fear, a habituated hiatus of any sound, an invisible nothingness awaiting the eventual noise before life itself forgets to stir. We feel the entire environment bracing for a sudden clatter, or some loud creature to suddenly break through the soundless stasis. It is finally howling wolves, the call of the wild, the beastly chorus that restores the sounds of night. A wild spirit has broken free to reanimate the audible world, saving us from this silence that struck too long. Showing all is alive and well, a communal pack howls this celebratory song, inviting other yearning voices gone too long quiet into their rounds of wolfen harmonies. We sing and howl at the top of our lungs, unashamed of who might hear us, where anyone may join in this night that is proudly and loudly ours.

108. A young woman dives off a cliff and hits her head but it's not that bad

A young woman stands at the precipice and dives off a cliff, throwing her entire self out into the open. Taking a chance on this steep possibility staggered with potential hazards, she leaps into this chasm of the unknown. She hits her head, but it's not that bad, and though some pain or other minor setback has probably occurred, the landing feels far from detrimental. The impact of her risky action has given her a fast boost of experience, and with this quick stammer of fright her eyes are opened a bit wider. She will approach her next great leap with a broadened periphery of insight, the memory of movement will guide her away from the mistakes of the first dive that caused her to hit her head. When we can realize little nicks and hits are "not that bad," we have the perseverance to continue on without the fear of falling down with a few bangs along the way.

109. A string of bells for miles chimes all at once

The sound rings along a string of many miles, pockets of music chiming all at once at the toll of numerous bells. Connected by the cord that links them together, they are resonant and tuned as one, individual clappers clinking their common song. The jangling wave of sound is far-reaching, a broad stretch of symphonic coordination that reaches people, animals, and spirits for miles. The chimes are quite a commotion, emotional and even holy, as we reminisce of steeples suspended over the earth ringing loud, a swell of bells that clangs into the refuge of our hearts. This cumulative string of song brings the aura of a climactic heavenliness, a powerful invocation where spirits make themselves known, striking a sound that must be heard.

110. Pouring bubbly drinks makes it sticky

Stickiness infers an adhesion that holds things together, in this case tacked by a fizzy drink. This is the sparkling atmosphere of a special occasion where something is certain to stick. The celebrated festivity is expected to attract some kind of bond, either a person as an attachment of interest, or a new concept or purpose we suddenly latch onto. A sticky situation could become messy if we overpour indulgent beverages, a caution against excessive consumption or oversharing things about ourselves we may later regret, warning us to avoid creating a reputation we do not want to be stuck with. In a positive light, we have this chance to establish ourselves by expressing and embodying the truths we want glued to our identity, telling the stories we want to be known by. The glistening effervescence that bubbles forth shows us that whatever we distribute or receive during this event is likely to stick.

111. An electric lightbulb fades in and out

Electricity and light ignite us, they literally fill us with energy and vision and create a field that enables us to see. This lightbulb fades in and out, buzzing on and off again, power surging and fading. Little bursts of clues and insight between periods of rest, inconsistent revelations of sight and then visual absence. The flickering light shows the long term power is dying off, but perhaps the strangeness of these obscure displays are revelatory with strobes of suggestion, granting little umphs of impulse for us to contemplate in the pauses of its dark rest. But as the intermittent insights become weak and show us the light no longer, it is time to replace the fizzled out parts with improved modes of brightness for our vision to remain sharp. After the ambiguity of contrast dwindles into a total absence of light, we must revamp our power sources to effectively fuel us into the future.

112. A naked tribe walks through grasses taller than they are

A naked tribe unashamed in their skin, their bare bodies stroked and brushed by tall grasses as they pass through the soft flowing cover. The kiss of dew from the unmachined, a natural safari leaves us appreciating the simplicity of this bare beauty. Far from domestication and stylization, we see everything in its natural state, unclothed and unmanicured, no intervention of labels or calculations. We honor a wild existence and hold a special place where these primal purities may live distinct from modern conventions, a free place in the wildlands of our hearts where there is no need for entertainment or adornment, naked and bare and basic, the fundamental rudiments of what remains when we strip all the embellishments away. In the image of the wild, taller, older, grander uncut woodlands and grassy tassels, we enjoy the most simple natural essence of our unobstructed selves, the gift of life in the pure form of our living breathing flesh.

113. A panicked man is hollering and no one can hear him

Whether this is ourselves or another person, there is someone who desperately needs help, and worse, is unable to effectively ask for it. This anxiety is festering in lonely chambers of futile hollering, zapping away what energy remains. We need to open our souls and ears to identify who or what is asking for assistance. If we find the need within ourselves, it is time to take different measures and change our ways of communication, perhaps more directly approaching friends to support us, or switching up our company to a place where we are more likely to find care and empathy. If we sense the need of another, we should check on those who might be vulnerable, and ask our loved ones or acquaintances if they need anything. It could be inspiring to seek out those who are definitely at a great disadvantage, or to those who are certainly suffering, and offer a helping hand. Though screaming with no one there to hear us is the stuff of nightmares, we can look forward to the relief once we've pulled the panic out from the trenches.

114. A woman walks alone in night streets singing

The woman needs no one else to make her feel secure in this moment where some may feel cautious at night on these dark streets all alone. Rather than hunkering down in fright, she announces her presence by singing as she walks, an expression of herself for herself beyond all judgement or fear. Being alone permits us to access our unfiltered inner realities and express them intimately to ourselves, a private interaction that gives us a firm foundation for communicating and presenting ourselves to the outside world. This solo stroll down the night street calls us to walk the paces of our freest spirit, a precious space for ourselves alone, our first ally before we allow anyone else inside. The carefree song we sing alone in the dark reveals to us what is stirring within, playfully informing us of our own inner secrets.

115. A woman gives birth in a bed of flowers

This aromatic image is lush with femininity and life, a bouquet of beauty, petals unfolding as birth blossoms. As the infant emerges upon this bed of flowers, the moist fragrance of fresh life is budding, the floral spread scented in celebration of the mother's womb. Laid upon silken flowers, the woman is honored as the source of all life, her lips and folds and dewy nectar, a center that opens to reveal her creation. As she gives birth, the satin petals welcome the infant, a perfume of flowers laced with the sweet sap of mother, the fertile fields of woman. This is an idyllic scene of beautiful birth, the woman and child are blessed. We praise the mother, Mother Nature, giver of all life, today and always.

116. A total blackness without even one starlight in the sky

A blanket of black has engulfed us, swallowed our sight. When one of our senses is paused or restrained, the others become heightened. In the saturation of this pure black, we suddenly hear every single thing and feel the slightest change of air. Our proprioception is skewed and we feel lost in space without visual cues of where to step and how to avoid tripping or stumbling. The best thing to do when we find ourselves in blackness is to relax into the situation and explore the audio sensations or the worlds of touch instead, or even just submit to the joy of our own imaginations drawn into the black. Immersed in total darkness we discover that our perception is the same no matter if our eyes are opened or closed, a visual correlative to how sound is to silence. Beyond the sight of our eyes, other worlds are available for us to perceive through a different kind of vision.

117. Tiny birds flying over vast oceans

Tiny birds flying over vast oceans is a profound expedition to visualize, the deep sea storms and grand miles of expanse offering nowhere to land, and nothing of the journey guarantees safety or ease. Despite the apparently formidable attempt of the tiny birds crossing such stretches, migration is indeed a part of their nature. Measuring up with counts of size or other crude analyses is a suffocating and limited way to read potentiality. Will, courage, instinctual calling, practice, tradition, or just inspiration arising within an individual or group, can all break through what might first seem technically impossible. The present voyage appears extreme but in truth it is strangely natural. These ambitious birds have set drafts as our precedent, and though the enormity of the flight makes the creatures look tiny, it is for this reason we must spread wide our wings.

118. The boot is ripped on the fence while running by

A reckless chase or a tough escape, a rugged jaunt or a recreational sprint, whatever it may be, these feet on the run have encountered a setback. Depending on the severity of the ripped boot, the degree of hindrance caused by this speed bump, the problem will need attention sooner or later. This is a clue that we should double check our footsteps, the conditions of the trails we tread, in which case the impediment serves us in the long run by checking our awareness. If the tear is more severe, and especially if the terrain requires shoes, the whole run has been disrupted, leaving us with the challenge of continuing on, dragging the half-functional boot through the snow if that's what it takes, tucking and tying the rip together as we can. A little slow down has interfered with our speedy spree, but the main goal now is to fix the problem as much as we can and continue on, neither to overreact nor ignore the little snare, and learn from what it tells us.

119. Two lovers trace each other's palm lines

These lovers expose to each other the intimacy of their sensitive pulse, palms open as they trace lines and patterns in this delicate study of the other. The supra electric nerve laden palm is a vital gateway to key energy lines that run through the entire somatic system of the body. As we run our fingers inside the soft flesh of our lover's hand, we touch a connection that reaches deep into their physical and emotional worlds. We surrender to this sweetly seductive experience as we give and receive unhurried caresses, smoothing our fingertips along the other's palm lines, interpreting maps and patterns and life stories. We let down our guard to mutually satisfy our desire to connect with the beloved in this sensual exploration of body and soul.

120. Ecstatic people dance with shadows

Shadows are the opposite side of what is apparent in the light, the elusive outline of ourselves, the black blob that mimics us and follows us as a strange featureless rendition of our bodies, separate from our form but still of it. Shadows contain our secret faces hidden in the dark, all that is concealed from exposure and finds domain in this negative space where there is no light. As our physical shadows continuously change according to the angle of the sun, our internal shadows are similarly distorted, cycling into awareness and then disappearing again into the void at high noon. Our secrets, guilts, fears, and regrets, all that is rejected from our waking conscious experience is suppressed and contained in the shadow, also casting blackness as a blind projection onto something that would otherwise be seen. This is an exhilarated dance of freeing and embracing the shadow, an ecstatic celebration to move with it and own it, accepting it as an aspect of ourselves, remembering that to have a shadow, there must exist light.

121. Someone levitates from a singing chorus

One impassioned singer stands out in the chorus, levitating in a euphoric climax of musical bliss. The shining individual's performance is extraordinary, uplifting the choir to new heights as the sonic ascension elevates the audience to greater peaks as well, the entire place floating on elated spirits carried higher by song. The talented savant of the chorus takes us to the pinnacle of musical magic in this unparalleled performance that invites everyone present to soar. Either the sound of our own voice is asking to sing freely or we are to listen and rise with the music that most moves us. A portal of transcendence opens the ethereal with this key of magical intonation, a spiritual experience where we levitate into the cantillation of this ultimate musical high.

122. The lizard runs in circles drawing spirals in the sand

The ancient reptilian lizard running in circles strikes us as a
motion of eternity, a depiction of the ongoing spiral. When a circle
shifts slightly with each overlap, when a new circumference is
repeated with a variant that makes the following circle offset from its
prior drawing, a spiral as a three dimensional tunnel emerges. This
image opens a gateway of time, an active portrayal of foreverness
exuded in this maneuver, a fixed energy steadily coiling into forward
momentum, past as a bridge to the future. The antique lizard, the
repetition of the endless circle, the progressive manifestation as the
eternal force in the spiral, and the elemental sands of time, all
connect to indicate a longevity in this action, a vortex that opens
through an indefinite portal. Whatever it is that accompanies the
quality of this moment holds promise for a long lasting existence.

123. A luxurious hammock is swinging but nobody is in it

A luxurious experience hangs unclaimed, teasing the interest of a
potential taker. Empty and unnoticed, the deluxe opportunity feels
somewhat remote, as if we must be clever to find the way to this
lavish leisure. Rocking its gentle invitation, the exclusive hammock
persuades us to imagine the dream destination where it swings. This
indulgence is not one of compulsive senses but is rather a call to
sumptuous respite. Once we arrive, the luxurious hammock lures us
in, coaxing us to relax and surrender to the cradle of the earth's
swing, allowing the gravity of our everyday burdens to release in this
moment. It is our turn to climb on and enjoy this special retreat of
quality rest, full permission is granted.

124. A woman lying on her back as a spirit comes down to kiss her

Laying supine we can view all directions at once, the dome of our world sky covers us as our back sinks into the earth. This woman has stared into the firmament, drifted with the clouds, risen in the rays of sun and moonbeams, connected with the sky. Her mental and emotional fluctuations have been left behind, exchanged for a celestial gaze filled with black jeweled nights and cerulean days. She drinks in the periphery, taking in the grand world sphere as an ascended spirit descends from his heavenly abode to kiss her. When we dedicate our impressions to contemplating the profound mysteries, the compatible spirit will notice our genuine awe of the gods and cosmos, and by some magic of this attentive kiss, we receive a gift only understood by ourselves alone and the divine source of love that has touched us.

125. A globe spins as someone searches for answers

Questions and answers are demanding attention in this revolutionary spin. All geographic possibilities and world contents are scanned in this search for direction. This person is in a quizzical state, clearly seeking imminent guidance as they read these signs of suggestion. There is a sense of sudden curiosity, a realized displacement, a need for reorientation, our world is asking to expand or change. With the scale of the entire globe as our parameter, this randomized search could transport us a significant distance. Whether we are taking a journey by actual travel or the venture is more of a studious nature, we prepare to broaden our vision into the scopes of the panoramic.

126. Everyone is laughing at the mockery in the middle of the room

An entertainer is the center of attention, either with comedic awareness or by playing the fool. The charade in the middle of the room is not the humor of baseless bullying, but is blatantly absurd. Everyone is laughing at this clownlike drama, which could be a humiliating drunken display or other means of ridicule if not intentional theater. Of all mammalian life, laughter is exclusive to humans as a part of our higher intelligent selves, and is strangely only partially voluntary. When we laugh, it has great effect on ourselves and others, and if we are indeed entertained it is one of the best joys, though it is equally hurtful if used to mortify. This situation is either full of goofy entertainment where laughter is our medicine, or an invitation to kindness by helping, if we can, spare the subject from unanimous embarrassment.

127. All of the angels descend into human beings for a brief effective moment

An overwhelming enlightenment befalls us, all angels descend into humanity in this momentary rush of glory. The event is described as effective, so the composite goodness of the angels has bestowed a heaven-born virtue and purity into our human souls, and knowing it transpires for only an instant, we hope to keep a small dose of the blessing forever. Human beings, halfway between animal and divine, have the primitive instincts of hunger and carnal appetites as our lower bodily functions, and from our heart upward we are moved by godly attributes such as love, empathy, compassion, and spiritual longing. During this period we are motivated by our highest integrity, the best places of our heart and mind, our moral consciousness as our leading guide, and filled with pure angelic light we ourselves at this moment host heaven within.

128. Hot metal sits heating in hot coals

There is an abundance of heat and it is growing…hot, heating, hot, and still roasting. We are careful to prevent burning ourselves, sure to remain aware of how we handle everything in our present space. Such high temperatures make metal first glow red and then become malleable as liquidized metallic fire, flexible and able to bend without breaking. In the same way tools and crafts are made by working this pliable metal, we too become more elastic when our own temperatures rise. The furnace is on and the heat is rising, and though we must beware of sparks and scalds, great transformative power is red hot and glowing, prepared for us to shape it in any way we choose.

129. Hiker adventurers are covered in pine sap

The adventure for these hikers has led to an aromatic slathering of pine sap. Each one will have a personal chemistry with the goo, some might find it irritating, while others will think of it as medicine, and a few will wipe it off or ignore it without much thought at all. Sticky with wilderness sap we tune into our native intuition to see if the ooze might be used as a healing salve of the wild, perhaps to repel insects or soothe an ache, or maybe just delight us with the pure fragrance of nature, our reaction implying how well we are constituted for what lies ahead. This is a preview, a taste of what's to come, an early measure that indicates how much we naturally belong to the place where we are going.

130. He steps over the hole of death but only sprains his ankle

The dark hole of death is averted, a serious close call has passed and a small crisis replaces an otherwise fatal catastrophe. Our present problem is an insignificant fraction of what could have been, this inconvenience is a blessing in disguise. As we suffer this minor injury, we are immensely grateful it was not worse. Downswings and setbacks come due for everyone and as long as the cycle delivers manageable troubles, we realize all is quite well, knowing that behind our difficulties there is always something much worse. This attitude will help us handle life's troubles with less complaint and with more resilience we will bounce back faster and stronger. Our journey is protected at this time and we are very much alive.

131. A hungry shark heads to shore

A monster predator from the cold sea is hungry for warm blood, heading directly to shore where humans are plenty. The destined beach towards which the shark is moving leaves all people unwittingly vulnerable at this time. Potential danger is coming our way and those most exposed are susceptible to attack, the shark being hungry with sharp teeth primed to pierce its next meal. We must keep open eyes and practice extra caution, staying closer to shore and away from the depths until the threat has withdrawn. It is a good time for intense observation of our surroundings, practicing wisdom and clarity to assess the intentions of those around us. Is something in our world hungry for us or someone we know as an unsuspecting victim?

132. Demons break up a worship ceremony but cannot get it

A demonic interference is beating at the doors, evil entities tearing their way through in an attempt to destroy the worship of good. Though diabolical forces have attacked, goodness prevails, a mysterious shield of divine protection has inhibited the malicious raid from stealing its power. This worship is so holy that the evil invasion cannot take down the strength of its divinity. The assault is deflected in the name of this immaculate ceremony, a sanctification so spirited that all we have to do is faithfully believe in its power to cast the demons away every time they try to break into our holy houses.

133. A musical genius composes their first piece

The conditions for genius have coalesced, a synoptic fusion of fate and will and practice is aligned and fully fit to house this powerful muse. A prolific time has begun for the newly confirmed, a masterful composer prepared to immerse themselves in the full language of the art. We consider the genius as a lucid medium directly connected to the cosmic well of inspiration and knowledge who is capable of transporting the highest arts and ideas from source into our world, expressing them with form and aesthetic as close to perfection as humanly possible. Imagining the brilliance of the genius we dream on the composition, a contemplation that vicariously links us to archetypal source, where the seeds of our own genius await our attention.

134. A saw cuts off the source of splinters

A problem is sawed off at the source, the lingering splinters promising to pester have been chopped away. We have detected an incubation site for repeated irritation, found the appropriate tool for dealing with the issue, and made a decisive act to cut it off. The image compels us to identify any bases of consistent pain in our own lives, anything that self-replicates as a continuous disruption, like the wood slab sewn with splinters. If we can uncover the source from where our sabotages spring and discern what relentlessly harms us, we see what we must be hacked off to eliminate predictable annoyance and discomfort. Whenever or wherever we find it, the pesky segment is cut away for good.

135. An anchor drops to the deepest point of the ocean

In order to reach the deepest point of the ocean floor, the chain must be inconceivably long and the anchor heavily fluked, such seismic proportions suggesting the sea vessel itself must be enormous. The cargo is ferried into the abyss, the ship moored above stores of subaquatic material and life, our own subliminal depths now semblant, nearly limitless. The movement of water sways with our emotional worlds of poetics and passions, all love and longing and feeling abides by the watery form. Anchored and secure, with the largest of all underwater worlds as our bearing, we dissolve into the tides of the moon and waters, fixed yet floating. As we drift in this expanse of great ocean, we are held and supported, ready to dive deep into our own watery worlds of emotion and feeling.

136. A comet restores faith in a hopeless teenager

This shimmering gift flashes a streak of hope across the sky and rescues this teenager from a state of despair. We are transported to a distant horizon as we witness the rare treat of a comet flying overhead, flung up and out of ourselves into the enchantment of outer space. Enraptured by this lustrous trail gleaming through the sky we shift into a brighter light that overtakes the urgency of our desperation. This comet arrives as a gift of strength, a flair of faith that shines through the dullness and pulls us out of our personal miseries and into a magnitude of higher knowing. The dazzling sky is resplendent with stellar phenomena that can uplift us in times of struggle, sporadic glimpses of hope ever fleeting by if we are present enough to look up and notice them.

137. A treehouse amongst cliffs holds stacks of books and a fireplace

A treehouse nestled into cliffs portrays an image both splendid and intimidating. It offers the beauty of staggering views yet there is a disturbing possibility of sudden collapse. The mood, however, carries little trepidation, rather we are coaxed into this warm atmosphere replete with stacks of books and a fireplace, a scene of enrichment and sophisticated pleasure. We feel cozy and welcomed to stay in this treehouse packed with knowledge and vast exposure, and as long as we remember we are on a ledge and step carefully along the ridges, there is much to learn. Being amongst cliffs we take in the mind-altering view, the reading material certain to live up to these heights with great themes that will inspire our inner vision as well. Traversing the ordinary, we are dared to find comfort in our risks, and charmed by our challenges we rise to this occasion of self-study to discover our highest selves.

138. A ring of people hold hands to guard a castle

A fortress is protected by a common people, hands clasped together in a gesture of defense. This ring of joined hands links them together in a continuous circle, unbroken energy beating through them as a collective warrior pulse. Together they stand facing every direction as they guard their stronghold, the shared set of values and culture that unite them. Determined to protect their castle, no trespassers or enemy will be able to pass without an earnest fight. In all battlefields, whether of war or those more subtle, we must be keen on what we regard as our sentinels and palaces within and without, and remain true to what principles and heritages we honor and protect. Whatever places or liberties we feel the present need to defend, we have a sphere of human connection that shares our cause. A group stands by, ready to take a solid stance to secure this communal treasure.

139. Water evaporates and invisible life drinks from it

We are taken across the threshold and into a domain beyond what we can see. Invisible life feeds on evaporated water, opening a pocket of unseen reality into a living and active world. It is interesting to note that water holds shape and retains memory, tiny vortices of its absorbed impressions as mini hurricanes within each drop. These cyclonic molecules carry a subtle vibratory message that in turn affects the cumulative charge of the entire body of water, as well as anything that drinks or grows from it. As with all energetic currents, water and otherwise, we know that the imprints we instill into everything we contact will be further assimilated in the perpetuum of all things, propelled onward into complex existences beyond what is visible. All things are feeding and influencing much more than what the limited world of the naked eye might lead us to think!

140. A child picks flowers for someone they bullied

Through the eyes of a child we experience a genuine remorse, inherent as natural kindness in the spirit of a healthy individual. While mistakes are inevitable, especially during the early stages of self-discovery and socialization, the most important thing is that we maintain the sane ability to honestly admit our errors, take responsibility, and apologize. In the phases of childhood development, there is an innocence that allows ample room for forgiveness, whereas an adult who still bullies becomes truly repulsive. Personality troubles along with plagued interpersonal relationships after the onset of maturity accompany the terrorizing life of the prolonged bully. This example of fresh picked flowers as a sincere apology from the child encourages an open space where we can make amends before the pathology of cruelty becomes a habit. It is important to keep a clean conscious slate and act as soon and authentically as possible when we realize we have caused unwarranted pain.

141. A small needle is lost forever in sand

A small needle is associated with delicate stitching, and our tool with which we've been mending has been lost forever in the sand. The work of the needle is finished, and whether it was completed with satisfaction or accidentally dropped, its job is done. In this moment of closure we realize something is officially irretrievable, tossed away into the peppered sands of all that has passed. If necessity demands, we might find a replacement tool to complete the work, otherwise it is time to abandon the task altogether and resist clinging onto something forever gone. Depending on how the needle was used, this loss could be momentarily difficult for us, or it may surprise us with considerable relief.

142. A plume of worrisome smoke turns out to be sacred smudge

A deep instinct triggered initial alarm, as where there is smoke, there is fire. Though the plume of smoke at first led us to believe destruction was blazing beneath it, it turns out the fire was not only unthreatening, but in fact sacred. Concern being our instinctual reaction assures that our primal defense systems are intact, and while we prove ourselves alert in the event of future danger, we also see how easily our perception and reasoning can be clouded as the smoke itself. We rest assured that the edge of our present anxiety is not as it appears but is actually derived from the opposite nature of what we originally assume. The billows arise not as a warning, but as a sacred smudge of holy herbs swirling as a gifted dose of protection and purification.

143. A pine cone falls and has a strangely long tumble down an endless hill

The pine cone tumbles in an endless descent, its seed-bearing scales rolling down this forever hill. Reproduction is perpetuating on every altitude, life spills down as the mature cone drops intermittent seeds in this long travelling implantation of the earth. The golden ratio is easily noticed in the pine cone's form, an extra layer of fecundity patterned into this image. What has blossomed and matured in the loftiest trees and the statures of our minds, has ripened and is readied for earthly descent. A terrestrial calling is fit to receive the released manifestation of our most well-structured dreams and inspired fruitions, what was once too high upon the canopy to touch is now within reach of the hands of the world.

144. Fluffy clouds host the real believer

As we rise into the comfort of heavenly hosts, the clouds show us that the spirit of belief takes us beyond the constructs of the material world. Sincere faith manifests as perceptions of body and mind, our emotions and our soul, a power so strong that if we imagine the weightlessness of the clouds, the soft touch of the fluff embracing us as we sit upon the sky, and wholeheartedly place our entire focus on feeling into this place, we begin to feel like we are in fact atop the clouds. This meditational experience renews us as if we had actually rested on the clouds, lightened as we return from this transcendental journey. Such sojourns to heaven give us a faith that takes us into the company of higher realms, the dwellers of the clouds who enlighten us so that we may manifest our visions in the truest ways possible. The ascension is real, we are taken beyond something physically possible, a belief so passionate, a visualization so clear that we meet it where it truly exists.

145. Women weave curtains for privacy from men

Feminine privacy is priority here, and the women create the opportunity themselves. They weave their own curtains to separate themselves from men and bask in the company of other women, or by themselves if they wish to be alone. It is a time for the women to flow in their feminine rhythms, allowing the watery waves of their

106

moods and emotions to run free without judgement or misunderstanding. These women are making a space to honor the intensity of feminine intuition, abundant passions and feelings not easily understood by rational assessments of logical diagnostics and solutions. This more masculine way of thinking can be a harmonizing balance to feminine energy, necessary in life as a whole, but during this particular moment each gender does well to recharge temporarily away from the influence of the other sex. Seeing here that they are only on opposite sides of the curtain, the separation is peaceful and respectful, mutually beneficial, though it is the women here who make the call.

146. A wild dog attack chases someone up a tree otherwise impossible to climb

On the run from a wild dog, nerves have kicked in and adrenaline is shot full throttle. Thrown into this sudden chase, survival mode turns on and all reserves of energy fire up to escape this attack. Supposed limitations are surpassed in this chase up the tree as we are driven to the edge of possibility, all expectations defied. The flight up the otherwise unclimbable tree is the ultimate display of latent potential forced into action by drastic desperation. Surprise situations as these on which our survival depends reveal to us our incredible stores of assets that lie dormant yet ready to utilize during such threats. Knowing such abilities exist within ourselves, perhaps we can intentionally draw from such reserves without the trigger of a crisis and use the energy willfully as we choose to accomplish what we assume to be too difficult or impossible. Whether by the pressure of necessity, or the driven passion of a far-reaching goal, we have what it takes to outrun the attacker and climb the daunting heights.

147. A woman hangs upside down for a new perspective

This alternative perspective is an inversion of everything familiar, usual circumstances flipped on their head. As the woman hangs suspended in midair she pauses to study the reversal of objects and processes in order to gain the insight she needs to best move forward when her feet are on the ground again. She surrenders control as her outlook shifts, making clear what at first glance appears illusory or irrelevant, and what remains centrally important during this play of perception. The insight attained during this moment of submission reveals to us our prior obstructions, blockages that required this inversion to realize. If we can set aside our resistances and see things from another perspective, we will feel the fresh blood flow to our head for a revitalized clarity. When we are soon upright, stuck and suspended no longer, our direction will be certain, new eyes thankful that the wait is over and we are on our feet again.

148. A magician teaches a rare disciple

A worthy pupil has been identified as a rare disciple ready for induction into this magical lineage. The official commitment of teaching has begun in this special time of initiation, the newcomer fully accepted and confirmed into this tradition as a life path. This transmission will stabilize and prolong this school of thought, and gives a new role to both the mentor and the student, the former now to crystalize and extract the most concise essence of the teachings, and the latter a profound responsibility to carry the torch. The trusted disciple will work to preserve the honor of the lineage by keeping its original wisdom intact while also updating the teachings to remain relevant to changing times, authentically and dutifully conveying the knowledge in a modern light and with the ongoing maturation of their own experiences. A bounty of wisdom and tradition is inherited, magical knowledge bequeathed to a successor, a rare disciple of great promise.

149. A mad person ties and unties knots

Knots tied and untied over and over again may teach us a thing or two about the many complex knots that exist, however this production is one of madness. Repeatedly doing and undoing the same thing we accomplish nothing except mental exhaustion, the strain of ceaseless effort with no real progress. The wasted dynamism of these hands with the deadened brain stuck on repeat bears no fruit, only the toxic habit of empty agitated work. Tangled and untangled again this person is unable to find their way out, restrained by the reappearing knot, yet once they untie it, it is they themselves who recurrently tie it up again. This indicates a robotic cycle of repetition, a futile busywork that gets one nowhere. A bad clash of overactivity and stagnation have programmed this dull reiterating nonsense. We need to tie the knot if it needs to be tied, or untie it once and for all, for in this preoccupation we are on the brink of madness. It is imperative we change our focus and break this

irritating and unproductive cycle, as the mad person warns in this
insanity.

150. A beach at night lit with rows of candles

Beauty and peace, water and fire as a perfect balance in this
tranquil yet vibrant night. Rows of candles insinuate a festivity, a
ceremonial gathering, or else a low key ritualistic connection of a
more personal nature. The glowing candles are strong enough to stay
lit in the airy ocean breeze, serene strength that perseveres in the
night. We feel the soft whip of the flickering flames banter with the
gentle crashes of the waves as they roll across the sandy shore, this
elemental wonderland evoking a deep aesthetic as the body of the
coast supports us. Rocked by the soft rushes of beauty in this
soothing natural paradise, we align with the quiet rumble of the night
waters and the stoic wicks that keep the small flames burning.
Tonight we are asked to do nothing but soak in the peaceful warmth
of the candlelight at the edge of the cool sea, resting yet invigorated,
embraced by the vital elements in motion around us.

151. Dry skin is quenched with bee balm

The skin as our outermost sheath has been quenched with one of
the most naturally potent forms of healing hydration. Bee balm is
brewed by the queens of pollination, the buzzing bees who instigate
the production of food for all living species, keeping the plant world
alive and reproducing, and therefore the world fed. We have
absorbed this splash of vitality into our own skin, enlivened by this

raw nourishment, and so we hope it penetrates into deeper layers of our being as well. Organic skin responds to organic moisture, a wholeness healing a wholeness, in no part botched or extracted or corrupted with additives. A reminder flies by that insists we avoid chemicals and harsh ingredients that are harmful to this living cycle, and instead feel this bliss of being truly quenched and healed from nutritive natural sources, one with the bees and all that is harmonious with this interwoven cycle of life on earth.

152. Young boys race each other laughing

This is a healthy scene of young boys testing themselves competitively in the supportive company of early friendships. These kids begin to experiment with where they stand in social structures as they identify their strengths and weaknesses in relation to their peers. As adults we are nostalgic for this lightheartedness before later failures and shortcomings may cause us to lose confidence despite the forward momentum life offers. The point is not to obsess on our comparative rank to others, but to allow the challenge to win to push us to up our game and improve ourselves in the process. By learning from those who finish ahead of us, noting new successful strategies and integrating them with our own effective methods, we can learn to only compare ourselves to ourselves and thus advance. In a ceaseless pursuit towards excellence we step into the race, head held high no matter how we place at the finish, knowing we will win something out of it, and with the spirit of youthful laughter, we will have a great time doing it.

153. A mystic briefly sees the laws of the universe

A mystic has accessed a powerful momentary perception of something far greater than themselves, a sublime connection of truth woven through the entire universe. There is a vision beyond our temporal senses, a brief flash of profound inexplicable knowing. The revelation of this seer stirs up visuals of sacred geometry as a spread of patterns for universal design, mandalas and the golden ratio radiating in and out of proportionate swirls. Everything as far out and huge as we can imagine refracts down to the tiniest microscopic particulates, through the deepest wells of our souls and all we can dream to envision and then back again into the grand scheme of the universe by some strange torus of energy difficult to fathom. Of course we are unable to rationally explain or confirm these mysteries but if we are sensitive to some of the clairvoyant energies that move in astral worlds that inevitably coexist alongside our own limits of perceptible frequencies, then we open ourselves to an awareness that gives us glimpses into the miraculous. We might find this a good time to explore such ideas in art, writing, or meditation to uncover and develop universal truths as we access and understand them deep inside ourselves.

154. An evolved reincarnation comes for a good person

This is a clear karmic ripening as a reward for habitual virtue from a previous lifetime, or earlier actions in the present life. A good person is not one who coldly cashes in quick deeds of merit, nor is a helpful person one who does so grudgingly. An evolved person gives with patience and care and is truthfully pleased to be of love and service, driven to do right from deep inside their private heart. For the sake of wide reaching wellness that includes our own, we do not seek praise or privilege as our motivation, nor do we only act virtuously so that our goodness as a rule is owed back to us, but we seek the sole reward of knowing that the peace and pleasure of authentic love and caring lives true to our very core. Perhaps if we always endeavor to live from this honest loving light, we will evolve towards the natural magnetics of favorable outcomes for both ourselves and those around us, in this life and beyond.

155. A butterfly escapes a spiderweb in the nick of time

The emblem of flying beauty and transformation, the exquisite butterfly, is caught in this sneaky sticky trap spun and tended by the spider who wants to consume it. The surprise of its translucent web tricked the unsuspecting prey as it flew by, so now the innocent must quickly realize the dangerous hold of this tight grip and flee immediately. It is our job to notice the butterfly is positioned to be devoured, and that without intervention its delicate beauty will be soon savored by this hungry spider. We are alerted to this vulnerable fragility, and whether we stumble upon this as a witness, or it is we ourselves at stake, there is one last chance to escape this trap in the nick of time. As the freed butterfly demonstrates, it is the strength of our own fluttering wings that must initiate this liberating flight.

156. Sea salt rubs away weeping poison

A combined excess of moisture, heat, activity, and toxic exposure has aggregated into a weeping poison. To establish balance once again we must apply opposite qualities to reverse the proliferation of these over-volatile dynamics. The drying property of sea salt is our perfect remedy, a granulation that neutralizes the poison and lifts it away from the skin. With luck we might directly enjoy bathing in the ocean waters, where the gentle abrasion of salt washes over our skin as the cool sea soothes our inflammation. Otherwise we may work with the salt alone and consider its source as we imagine the healing lull of the waves and the slow liquid density of the supportive ocean. When we stray too far from a stable center, problematic imbalances surface and spread, and to avoid this we must recognize their qualities and administer harmonizing opposites. With this soft exfoliation of the ocean's touch, the inflammation is tamed, our weeping poison dries away and troubles us no more.

157. Gardeners sift compost with their hands

These gardeners are in direct connection with naked raw natural life as the bare touch of their hands sift the earth, crumbling the clumps of compost with their ungloved palms. This immediate contact pushes loving energy into the soil, the heart of thoughtful touch adding to the work. By breaking down the compost we make it more digestible for the garden, so in the same way we can make our nurturing energy more accessible to everything in our greater process, everything we choose to touch. The attentive gardener witnesses the superior health of plants tended with caring hands. The quality of the material, the compost, as well as the energetic imprint distributed by the touch of our skin, become the germs of energy that are fed to the plant, and then become the plant, an impression that progresses through cycles of growth and decay. Such an intimate interaction gives us the opportunity to mix with an organic exchange of natural energy, fortifying ourselves and our gardens and all the land. We are enthusiastic and ready to get our hands dirty! Mud bath anyone?

158. A mother tells her child to make a wish

Any maternal blessing that opens the way for a wish is auspicious, and what the loving mother invites forth we hope is granted. As awesome as an answered wish might be, it is a big responsibility to choose it well, should it come true. It is imperative that we are wise with the wish and first examine all aspects of the imagined outcome. Of course it is easy to have many impulsive wishes, but with the request being for a child, this is an invitation to dream up an entire life trajectory, blessed by the early support of the mother. We must be sharp enough to envision the subsequent effects of our wish that will build the series of events that make up our life. If we are clear enough to imagine the unfolding of this ongoing dream gratification as a prolonged fulfillment, we might have enough insight to pinpoint where it all began.

159. A pocket too heavy breaks open

We are hauling around too much, our pockets have ripped at the seams. It is time to take personal inventory, examine our baggage, and decide how to lighten our load. As a point of reference, we must first check in with our incumbent responsibilities and those we have voluntarily taken on. Then we move onto our false burdens, both imaginary pressures and those we impose onto our lives that are not relevant or required. We must identify and eliminate superhero syndromes where we might unnecessarily insist on helping in areas where it is not wanted or needed. Once these are cleared, we scan our physical possessions and see if we are running ourselves in circles by having too many things that require cleaning or tiresome upgrades or that primarily function as needless distractions. After we discard unnecessary weight, we can take a fresh look at our cargo and find ourselves much more at ease with regard to what we choose, or are obligated, to carry. If we feel satisfied with our load, finding nothing fit to remove, perhaps it is time for a sturdier coat with bigger pockets.

160. A champion of peace sends a message in a bottle

A message of peace has floated into the abyss, sent adrift with apparent aimlessness. Inside the bottle, a champion's call to peace is a pending proclamation that awaits discovery, its destination undetermined, some potential peacetime hovering in a sealed capsule that is not yet ready to open. This elusive bobbing around of such esteemed writing imposes a looming suspense, a great unread message lingering that must be found. The importance of the message urges us to seek it, ennobling us to receive the idea into our mind as we imagine the contents of what we would write or what we have read or would expect to read from peaceful prophets we admire.

We listen to the vague whispers of peaceful champions until we flow into the current where their messages are carried, perhaps ourselves capable of deciphering and enacting the meaning of the lost message that awaits its revelation.

161. A woman at the peak of her beauty ties her hair back

This is a look into exquisite motivation, an exposition of the ripened beauty of a physically lovely woman who exudes a lively vitality. She is tying her hair back as if it is time to get busy and move, prepared to work towards her peak accomplishments. Her prime confidence shining, she exposes her face, pulling back her hair to reveal a smile or an openness that makes available the expression in her eyes. She is approachable and presents a willingness to communicate, to persuade and perhaps be persuaded. Aligning with the cadence of this woman, we feel fresh and energized, ideally positioned to reap the benefits of our assets, and now facing forward with grace we proudly approach our greatest ambitions.

162. A love letter is written but they get a paper cut

Anyone sliced with a papercut after writing a love letter will naturally wonder if it signifies a greater implication. There is a conflict between the passionate letter and the sting of the cut, and though the cut is minor, there still may be a reactive yelp, some onomatopoeia of pain that punctuates the writing. A jab of negativity might follow, we feel a tinge of mockery after this declaration of love, and it may in fact be a premonition of pain to come. However, with a deeper look, the spirit of passion could have induced this small sacrifice as a magical signature, a seal of love. The trace of blood was shed in the very rhythm of the beating heart that wrote the letter, the pulse carried further into the message. It is these subtle signs that are for us to read as magical guidance, intuitive interpretations that confirm or deny truths within, things that only we may answer for ourselves, what compels us to love and live an enchanted life.

163. Wild animals running freely on open plains

We are called to head outside and enjoy the open air, the joy of running as living breathing moving life. Unbounded on wild plains, there are no roads or gates or fences, no finish line, no lanes, no rules to our play. Wildly free and fast we relish our physical form, the capacity to move, the fluid articulation of joints. How exhilarating to use the perfect aerodynamic form of our animal body, agile muscles perfectly wrapped around sturdy bones to propel us into action with astounding precision, our beating heart pumping blood through our veins that give us oxygen and nutrition, and as we race around this open field we viscerally feel what a marvel life is! With fierce mammalian joy we experience our form in the best way our body allows, finding the truest movements of our own inner animal. Spontaneous energy calls us to embrace this exalted motion, finding our way as far as we can off the beaten path to frolic and play, and with animal stamina we are ready to run!

164. A holder of wisdom writes down secrets

A wisdom holder has made secret teachings accessible, the written form manifest and therefore readable and available for discovery. Authoring such material is a great responsibility, ideas become immortalized, verbatim in the content of the written word. Not only must the bearer of these secrets effectively elucidate the core essence of the important wisdom as to not mislead or distract from the main teaching, but also to omit or only carefully hint towards sensitive knowledge that becomes easily misunderstood or misused, that which may be only experienced and understood for oneself. There is authentic perennial wisdom that must be preserved and shared as a contribution to humanity's body of knowledge, works to be approached with the highest respect. Secret wisdom is held in sacred collections, texts and concepts shared only with those who are sincere and prepared to receive the knowledge. Anything written begins a life of its own, so we are wise on what we choose to crystallize as truth by word.

165. A young warrior is ceremonially pierced

The young warrior has advanced into a new stage of life, there is a change of identity. This is a rite that celebrates a coming of age or a battle victory, the warrior ceremonially pierced to mark this official passage into the next phase. A piece of childhood innocence is left behind, the warrior has stepped into a role with a new purpose, dependent no longer on the caregiving of others, serving now as a protector of the tribe. The piercing gives the warrior recognition through the public display of initiatory rite, a declaration that they are

119

strong enough to handle pain, ready to face the world and respond to any battles that might call. In our own symbolic gesture we bravely we step forth and away from the protection we've outgrown, ready to walk tall and handle our own challenges, celebrating the warrior we have become through this initiation.

166. Old wooden wheels stuck in asphalt

Old wooden wheels have a rickety and rough connotation yet they also feel well-worn and comfortable, trusted and familiar. The wheels that have been so long reliable are stuck in asphalt, a trudge resistant to the future. We need an umph to get us through the sludge and moving forward again, the wheels need to get rolling either by replacement or repair. The times are changing so our tools and materials must be adequate for what lies further down the path. If we do not like the progression of the journey and wish for our old trusty wheels to live on, we may need to change course to avoid this particular road. We carry on with the old reliables as they can be kept, though we also understand that when things outgrow their utility, we must adapt to new solutions. As we ride the rotary on the wheels of time, we preserve the rustic as we are able and move forward as we must.

167. Curious people sort out rocks, shells, and fossils

An interested mind full of curiosity is a hallmark of a happy healthy person. An active mind that loves to learn and seek new experiences stays elastic and receptive, open to new ideas they are always discovering. People are sorting through clues of prehistoric life in these petrified piles of mineral and bone, from ancient fossils to shells freshly fallen from crustacean backs, gleaning through these deposits as a trail through time. Studying such vestiges of the past allows us to contemplate these relics as time stamps, a thread of life story that informs us of an organic process. By putting pieces of the past together to make the entire timeline more cohesive, we can better understand where we are in the present, inquisitive enough to interest ourselves in an engaged and curious future.

168. Ink is spilled and something beautiful is created

An alternative attitude is necessary to reveal this beauty, an unordinary reaction to the otherwise irritating accident. The success of this creation is not planned or measured, but is the result of an unwanted spill, a design that emerges without an artist. Although it might be messy, our usual methods of control may be temporarily abandoned in this chance to observe the outcome of something that happens on its own, especially if inconvenient. The ink is sure to stain wherever it flows, so in our observation we focus not on what is ruined but on what strange beauty unfolds from the otherwise annoying situation. With the willful practice of such response, we develop the skill of converting small problems into positive extractions pulled out of the inevitable. This allows us to avoid overreacting to small troubles, instead seeing them as creative opportunities that challenge us to morph the blotch of ink into the beautiful shape we find inside.

169. A pensive inventor ponders the next move

The brilliant creator is in the action of materializing the next great idea. Though the development is underway, the inventor pauses to consider its course. We are offered an innovative moment to strategize our direction at this crossroad. The project is open for a new interpretation, possibly requiring a new solution to proceed. This is a break to ponder our options and review the vision of the final outcome before we continue our work. During this hiatus we listen to inspired waves of ideas that may be our genius directing our way forward. Though this brief review is needed to keep us on track, we must also ensure that we do not slow our invention to a halt, but to instead return to our creation with ideas taken to the next level. This oscillation between thought and action will equip us to achieve the best original work we are capable of offering as our own unique gift.

170. A magnifying glass skims over a globe

With the entire global scale represented as the big picture, we are asked to look closer into specific areas regardless of their size or influence. This is not a time to generalize or dilute views into a blurred spin of the globe, but to take the magnifying glass and pay attention to distinct zones. As we skim over the world sphere we notice and appreciate the differences and similarities that span our globe, especially what is often overlooked or simplified. Diverse viewpoints are to be considered at this time as we celebrate other cultures and places and listen to each other's concerns and respect our fellow beings, enjoying our differences and admiring one another's strengths. In this moment of widespread examination and curiosity we study the wonders of the natural world and its people, every inch of the earth, every single person, completely unique and unlike anything else.

171. A family finds joy juicing berries with their hands

This family occasion induces laughter and joy, a healthy and playful experience that bonds them. The inky reds and purplish blues of the berries saturate their hands as the bright colors vividly emerge in our own minds. We join them as we feel the life in our veins awaken, pumping with vitality as colorful as the berries we squeeze. The senses are filled as we see the bursts of color splashing into cups, the sound that promises the taste of the sweet juice to come. Along with the nutritive reward of the rich vitamins and antioxidants, we have also infused a spirit of loving fun into the juice, an elixir to quench our every layer, from spirit to body, back to spirit again. We receive this and gather our loved ones to prepare an organic creation together, a recipe that calls for color and joy.

172. Blue birds land on a tiny island no one knows about

First we consider 'no one' as meaning that the island is unknown by human beings, in which case we imagine the vastness of life and beauty that exists there. As humans we are often ignorant of significant realities, from the physical spectrum of rare terrestrial abodes and microscopic life forms to our perceptual limitations, frequencies and dimensions we cannot know due to our sensorial restrictions. In this light the island evokes a sense of awe and imagination, a wonder towards the beautiful unknown that invites us to dream into these worlds we have never considered. Once we imagine this island, it becomes in some sense real, a sanctuary where these blue birds land in this gathering of their own kind. The tiny mysterious place conjures a mood of secrecy, a private meeting or a fleeting chance of possibility we happen to witness. We are away from the surveyed world, so whether through introspective imagination or by following the blue birds to their secluded island, this remote place sings of the birds' song, asking us to find it.

173. Two sticks finally spark a fire after a long time

The grind has been long going, and the two sticks have finally caught fire. This diligent tending has officially sparked, promising a full combustion shortly to follow. The fire must remain stable, it needs to be fed and sustained but not too much or it will take a destructive turn. With control we are faithful to the flame for as long as we wish, ever-attentive while allowing for oxygen and space so that the fire can breathe, maintaining the panting flicker that ensures it is alive. As with all fires, including those of the heart and passions, of the working disciplines, the transformations as the stove cooks and the bonfire disposes, we strive to maintain a balanced heat that warms but never scorches. The patience has paid off, the persistent friction has ignited the flame, the fuel of the light is burning and now we must choose what to do with it.

174. A scalpel removes a deadly growth

There is a cringe of pain as we anticipate the cut of the knife, but this scalpel is what saves us. The malignant growth is sliced away, detached from our being at last. Though discomfort is endured, it is essential to sever this deadly fixture. It must be cut away. Once it is removed we might examine the contents of the excised growth to inform ourselves of the fatal conglomerate we'd been accruing. If we know our enemy we can prevent its reinvasion, educating ourselves on how we best banish the problem and protect ourselves from serving as its host. Whether of spirit or flesh, this toxic attachment is cut away, and freed from its noxious grip we are clear again. Saved from this lethal scare, our life is instead lengthened, a renewed condition of optimal health and wellness.

175. A girl speaks promises out loud as she braids her hair

The girl weaves her declarations into the rhythm of her hair. This is a magical energy, words spun into the vortex of the winding spiral as she braids. A current is tangible, a live stream of promise vocalized as she handles her hair as if the protein structures are extensions of her inner mind, tying her intentions together and fabricating their reality. If we can speak our own affirmations with such conviction and promise, simultaneously working them into a creative gesture with our hands, we can further encode our wishes and intentions into the fabric of physical existence. In the way of the braid we artistically twist our hopes into being as we speak them into the universal vibrancies that coincide and work through spiral movements, good intentions, and hands of the magician weaving thoughts into creation. We propel thoughts into form this way more than we realize, our words and actions as the great woven tapestry that braids together our life.

176. A window rusted shut breaks open

Though the development of rust was gradual, its tight clasp suddenly bursts open in this fast and extraordinary change. Fresh air blows away the stench of long stale moisture that has sat too long as dank potential. The dormant energy held down by this corrosion has been whipped clean by a new breeze, an inspired ventilation that provides the ultimate refresh. Atrophied no longer, this dramatic renewal replaces what was tarnished with the glean of a new shine. As the translucent window is a two-way exposure, this enlivened aeration now seamlessly flows with clarity between our inside and outside worlds, and with this flush of vital breath we are now free to do whatever we choose, the window of possibility wide open.

177. A long fishing line cast off a tall balcony

This is a monumental feat, a long shot to attain what we seek. The height of this vantage point, however, offers us a broad range that covers much water, a big surface into which we can cast our line. Because the landing area is so wide we must be cautious to not accidentally bait something we do not mean to lure, thus requiring our focus to be extra sharp from this distant balcony. With regard to whatever we pursue, we are instructed to operate from afar, with plenty of space between ourselves and our target. Tools and gear serve us in this distal endeavor, so it is crucial we use the right equipment and have a keen eye for accurate retrieval, remaining steady to not topple from this advantageous pedestal. If we proceed with care for the waters at large and aim for what will sustain us without disturbing the greater sea, we are set up to reel in a win.

178. Two evils burn each other out in a fight

The hero is not needed in this scenario, a force for good is irrelevant in this self-extinguishing battle between two evils. No well-meaning person should intervene in this dueling malice, an infernal combat that incinerates the evil entities by mutual destruction. While there are certainly times when the hero is welcome, prayed for, this is a fight where the bad rips apart the bad, when goodness should standby intact, unharmed and fully ready for when the demand for savior presence does come due. For now, no energy is to be wasted on behalf of benevolence as the fuel of evil burns itself to the ground. We must only stay out of the way as the hellfire self-consumes with no loss to the righteous.

179. A god designs a new bush of spices

Fresh energy, a pang of flavor is alive and growing. Of divine design, this is the prime picante, a worthy spice fit for the gods. The bush beckons our desire to taste of its heavenly zest, to sample its tang and take in its aroma, where we may rise with it to a higher place of stimulated senses. We yearn to absorb the full gift of this new creation, tasting that which has never been tasted before. This new culinary sensation brings with it a renewed appetite for life, a gusto that revs up our excitement, something that truly feeds us with and beyond this palatable pleasure. There is an aspect of appreciation naturally incumbent in this gift from the gods, so with respect to the creative divine energies along with those that seeded and sustained the plant's growth, we nurture the bush, harvest with care, fully indulge in and enjoy its deliciousness, and follow up such delight with sincere gratitude. These steps of a widely applicable cycle give us a chance to season all we ingest with enhanced fervor and joy.

180. A child first discovers their spirit animal in a dream

The dream world is a place we wander outside of our bodies, where we fuse with our higher faculties of spirit and find missing pieces of ourselves. Deep seated realities, mundane or magical, are explored in the dreamscape, especially when experienced with the open mind of a child. By aligning our astral body with our closest animal allies, we are able to identify this spiritual totem and integrate it into our authentic spirit during the dream. This acquisition then follows us into our waking life, a force that streams through us as our wildest selves, our freest inclinations that climb and fly, howl and hunt, leap and swim, all the primordial qualities that satisfy a longing to embody and sing out as our inner animal. An asset from the dream world meets the child within and initiates us, healing our tender human heart with this feral source of courage and strength, the gift of the spirit animal.

181. Two people pulling bundles uphill with ropes

The necessity of rope indicates a heavy uphill load, but with the helpful support of coordinated effort, the haul is underway. One with our freight, there is no confusion of what we carry, the challenge of ascent keeps us aware of every pound that comprises the bundle, small cumulative weights making the difficulty more drastic than flatland transports. We are given an opportunity to examine the relevance of the bulk we drag, to ensure everything we lug around is useful to us in some way. Sincere effort is conveyed in this ambitious image, a purpose driving the two people and their cargo up into a higher destination. This undertaking requires extra pull and hard work, and with the support of a companion we remain steady on this ascent. Having not yet arrived, we are in the center of the action, determined to carry on. We look forward and climb, hands firm on the ropes, and do not let go.

182. A peaceful woman wrestles with a ghost

There is a silent conflict in the peaceful woman's internal processes. As the ghost is without form she too operates beyond what can be seen, visually at ease yet she quietly battles within. A shadow self seems to be stalking the psyche, likely as ruminations of unresolved miseries or regrets. It could also be true that this really is a visitation from some floating ghost who demands acknowledgement, apology, or release. Though we work to subdue such harassments and invasive thoughts we also must prevent repressing our shadow side, realizing the need to recognize our struggles before they are buried to our detriment and haunt us as ghosts. Each person's inner self is a unique private personal lens from which we view and interact with the world, so every invisible battle is specific to us alone and therefore our own responsibility to confront. When we successfully defeat or reduce our struggles with these problematic ghosts, our peaceful stature will reach beyond form, filled with the rich inner serenity that chases ghosts away.

183. A rock wedged into a tree opening

The tree is the grandest manifestation of the plant world, the highest source of earthly wisdom that invites us to grow with it, to teach those who wish to learn. Being the symbol of ever rising access to universal knowledge, the tree offers its winding footpath to those who wish to climb however high they dare to go. The opening in the tree suggests a receptive space available for something new, a stable rock, firm and unyielding wedged into the gap. This solid fit is suited to stay for a while, a steady contrast to the ever sprawling life of living branches. Though the rock is removable for now, the tree will eventually grow around it and take it into its center as a permanent core. As we ascend through life like the magnificent tree, we take this moment to find the rock solid firm foundations inside of ourselves, what were once separate yet became so familiar that we grew around it. We notice the stable constants that are unchanging within, those that stay the same as we continue to mature. The rock wedged into the tree opening is still on the surface, asking that we either remove it now while we can, or accept it as a long term support that will continue to move deeper and deeper inside.

184. A gold coin flipped

The prosperous golden coin has flipped, a reversal in the domain of wealth or resources. The coin is still in possession, so the treasure has not disappeared altogether but turned over to reveal another face. Our vision of worth has resurfaced in an opposite manner, a shift in how we regard our assets and power of purchase and trade. A change has occurred in the way we recognize true wealth, what we find rewarding and meaningful. How we prioritize our efforts and invest our time creates our occupation, what we seek and therefore value, and the energetic outcomes that follow these accumulations become our net worth. This flipped coin is an opportunity to purify and reassess how we define wealth, what genuinely gives us personal fulfilment of the highest value, the truest gold.

185. Pounding mallets to build structures

We hear the rhythmic pounding of hard work, a call to action. This laborious task is repetitive and manual but necessary to build a sturdy foundation for what this space of potential will eventually house. It is time to get busy and work with our hands to lay the initial groundwork for the later stages of our vision's full culmination. The rewards of these efforts are yet to come, so instant gratification is not likely. Before the activities and events of our highest dreams are effectively realized, we must prepare a durable platform that can support and sustain our future fruitions. We must dedicate ourselves to the prerequisite labor involved before the actual production may ensue, for if we are lazy and ineffectual in the bones of the basic structure, what is built upon it will be no good and it will not take much for the whole thing to collapse. We are prepared to sweat and exert our very best while maintaining an attitude of patience and a high standard in the quality of our work, for the level of excellence we put into the structural support directly affects everything that follows.

186. White ashes spread by the wind

This is an energetic gust, the source of roaring heat that preceded the white ash becomes mutable in the speedy wind. The transformed fuel as ash propels the energy onward, spread by wind where it will nurture new forms of life as it scatters over the earth. Anything that was so actively hot still holds this vital energy as stored potential, remaining viable and available for transfer when the right stimulus arrives. Such pauses are needed between energy conversions because if the ashes are spread while they are still too hot, destructive embers may ignite again rather than fertilize new life. If we use this transfer of power wisely, we can transmit the formerly active heat into vigorous nutrient-dense ash to feed vegetation, strengthening earth's foliage and thus fortifying the entire circle of life. This is a potent chain of volatility worthy of our focus, energy as a transmuted substance prepared to spread and settle, to consecrate new life.

187. Curtains fall, a naked woman in the window

The dramatic enticement of this sensuous unveiling excites us with surprise as the curtains fall and a naked woman appears. Separated by the window, the woman is alluring but untouchable, and we honor her by admiring her only as much as she wishes. In the case of an unknowingly spied on woman who believes herself private, such voyeurism is greedy and likely insulting to the woman who wants to reveal herself only at times and in ways of her own choosing. The subtle communications of her observer will influence the woman's responses, and if she senses a respectful approach, she might playfully dance in a sexy correspondence, perhaps even stepping out from behind the glass. However if we are greedy, betraying what we know is right, we should listen to our conscience if it tells us we need to turn away. Only by respecting woman do we know how to proceed.

188. A girl brushes and saddles her horse for a long journey

The girl has developed the skills to care for her horse both as a soulful companion and as her dutiful escort. Lovingly brushed and proficiently saddled, they are soon ready to depart as one on this fated journey. Rider and steed together embark on this coming of age mission where the girl seeks experience to guide her into future direction. The youthful velocity of ambitious pursuit bodes well for this long expedition, a regal strength and a good farewell full of high hopes. With our sturdy horse saddled beneath us, a charge of confidence thrusts us into the unknown, a path laden with adventures sure to shape us.

189. A wanderer finds their place and becomes a hermit

Motion and change have subsided, a lostness has become found. A substantial grounding has stabilized a prior state of wanderlust, this former nomad now firmly connected to a solid place. Frequent travels were previously necessary to stretch the limits of the self and find bearings in ourselves through the variabilities as the places around us were changing. Now this yearning is satisfied, our priority has shifted from wandering through temporary affairs without traction to establishing a deep relationship with a single place. Rooted with new purpose, the drifter is called home to concentrate on personal development and the miracles of life best observed from a steady place, the seasons and flora and views of the sky always shifting. The hermit calls for us to enjoy this undistracted solitude and ground ourselves, and at least for a while observe from this stillness, the world always turning whether we participate or not.

190. A witch coven meets at midnight

Convening between two worlds, this coven of thirteen at the time of twelve, with the certainty of darkness we are deep in the night. Thirteen represents the number of lunar months in a year, the feminine clockwork that directs natural growth and tides as well as the woman's own monthly cycle, whereas twelve is a solar time keep, society ticking by the tock of the imperfect manmade clock. A full coven is comprised of thirteen witches, their lunar energy brought into midnight as they tap into the rhythms of the moon and planets under the night sky, time signatures of their own that refute conversion to the clock as we know it. Authentic witchcraft aligns with natural cycles and basic elements to work with raw forces of energy brought forth by invocation. Our own magical inclinations find expression at midnight when the psychic air is cleared of everyday life, making the occult powers more available to those who conjure them.

191. Autumn leaves turning color

Autumn is the peak harvest and the onset of vegetative decline, the waning of the life cycle. Despite the oncoming chill, the sun is still high in the sky, summer heat persists and the pinnacle of growth is still hanging with rich fruit. The leaves are splashed with color, each hue perfectly distinct, every form unique in nature's way. Vibrancy is sustained in these colorful spectrums, the vitality that persists at the end of the season. Life is not quite ready to fade away, and before they dry and fall the leaves display their finest. We steep in the joy of this beauty, preserving these fantastic colors deep into our soul's memory, perhaps capturing them with photography or paint. As the reality of the inevitable winter freeze comes closer, this natural beauty reminds us to delight in it while it lasts, because as these leaves are soon to fall, we remember nothing lasts forever.

192. The top story of a house falls

A collapse from above, the top has become too heavy for the scaffolding that supports it. We can prevent another downfall if we realize its cause and correct the underlying mistake. If we discover that we have a weak foundation on stilts that buckled under light pressure, we need to bulk out the skeleton and add some muscle to our supporting beams. If the structure itself is satisfactorily strong but we find it was overburdened, we need less weight the top. We might be hoarding too much in the attic, or carrying too much in our minds, some top heavy mass has smothered us, leaving us with a need to reassess our points of balance. Whatever has toppled down must be built up again, strong enough to hold the weight we bear, material, psychological, or otherwise.

193. Dungeon doors snap open

A subterranean prison, eerie and dank with dragons and demons prowling. The doors of this hellward vault suddenly snap open, offering a chance to run from this agonizing purgatory, the iron clasps of enormous suffering are released. This escape may be from personal demons, freed and forgiven of guilt and self-inflicted tortures alive only in our own head. We are excused and no longer bound to any kind of abusive captor, be it ourselves or the oppression of the world. Rushing to the surface from the depths of darkness can be shocking, we may tremble as we search our way forward, but the return to light has come at last. It might take time before we feel normal again, to adjust to the light after being kept cold in the blind captivity of the underworld, but as we slowly adapt and let our confidence return, we have faith that our senses will learn to trust again.

194. A group of people lost in a maze

A misguided herd mentality has steered the group off course, the path to the destination is muddled and dizzy. Fresh insight is needed to navigate this maze, a leader needs to step up, free thinkers must gather their individual ideas until they can map their way to the exit. This is where the novel thinking of a bright individual can lead others to liberation, for when people work together and listen to those with insight, such cooperation can inspire many pioneering minds. It is easy to follow others blindly into confusion but it takes both courage and innovative tenacity to lead the lost into the right place. Spun out in this maze, we take a look at how we are letting mass thoughts infiltrate our own sense of direction, a chance to recalibrate. A clear orientation that will get us through the labyrinth is one where we think independently for ourselves, asserting with certainty when we do know, and with discernment we open up to the guidance of others when we do not, endeavoring to function always from a centered place that makes sense in our own mind.

195. A man tries to stop a wheel from spinning but can't

Like this spinning wheel that cannot be stopped, life itself is a continuous progression of moments always passing. The wheel of life eternally turns as certain as the planets orbit without pause. Our own experiences revolve round and round again, spokes radiating from the central hub of our lives, imprinting everything we touch on our path. We cross ways and exchange impressions with endless other vehicles, also constantly rolling ahead on their own tracks, all interwoven and spinning together in this ephemeral wheel. The man who tries to catch the wheel is grasping for the impossible, a useless attempt to stop time and prevent inevitable advancement of the cycle's continuum. Understanding the futility of such efforts, we attain peace by riding the wheel as it rolls, steering it with our will as we are able while making the most of the ever-changing scenery and surprises along the way.

196. Mushroom mycelium mixing with tree roots

This underground interdependence is an intricate lifegiving network of tiny threads that has enormous effects on terrestrial life. Connective tissue of the earth, mycelium is a fungal organism that can reach for miles, joining single plants together with a shared system of communication, defense, and nutrient distribution. This sprawling mycorrhizal life intermingles with their roots to nurture trees with water and minerals and protect them from invasive species that could otherwise colonize and destroy them. The prominence of this concealed life below the dirt is much like the complex existence we contain under our own skin, and humans too connect by invisible means similar to mycelium. As a tree can warn other trees a mile away of an oncoming threat, or give the go ahead to fruit because the benefits are rife, human beings communicate with hints of pheromonal scents and cues that evade our superficial conscious awareness. These miraculous energetic pathways exemplify the interconnectedness of all life, and inspire us to contribute our best loving essence into the shared network of living consciousness.

197. A waterfall builds stacks of foam

The flow of the waterfall remains constant, yet each drop that falls and every bubble that emerges and disperses is always changing. Foam develops from the pressurized mixture of air and water, stacks of it built by the impact of this enduring rush. Every bubble contains an etheric store of vital energy within, a kinetic endurance that perpetuates with the ongoing flow of the fountain, a descending force that pours into the earth and generates profound motion changing the landscape without human cause. The water itself is fleeting, but the power behind the falls is ever present. In this great cascade of foamy waters, we reach for a ripple of the frothing force and inseminate ourselves with this vital rush.

198. One with too much on his back sets some of it down

A sigh of relief as this person relieves their burden. The overbearing load is instantly lightened and we have permission to do the same, the decision has been made. Whether it is energetic or material, we have carried a heaviness that requires a break, if not permanent release. We are directed to examine the contents of outdated or cumbersome loads, whatever we are hauling around that hunches us over as we walk the world worn down and weary, that which keeps us closed off to new opportunities. Once these accumulations are peeled away, we stand up straighter and with a lighter spring in our step we walk on, freed into the future.

199. Two fruit trees grow twisted around each other

The intertwining of these fruit trees is a display of loving magnetic in the most natural way. The two of them twisting around each other is a long term attraction as they wrap higher and higher, branches interlacing like the limbs of compelling lovers growing ever closer. Inch by inch they move towards and away from each other again in a spiral lengthened and strengthened over years. Rather than fully grafting together, they remain individually distinct allowing for fresh air to flow between them, a constant purification that maintains free space as a clear healthy channel for pollination and vital energy exchange. This moves us to look at our own companions who have grown alongside us, from those who started as young saplings to those who leaned into our lives at a later point, just as these fruit trees have twined together in a high heavenly arch, a clasp beholden. This organic rapture of fruitful embrace is a sensuously woven arborary of two, together for life.

200. A non-receiver accepts a gift

This acceptance is the sign of an opening heart. As a non-receiver, this person is typically emotionally closed off and denies much of what others attempt to give. Until now this shutdown has caused great disturbance in the spirit of the individual, but it is time to change. Of course we must learn to receive for the benefit of our own sense of human connection, but also out of respect for the one who gives. To refuse a gift is to disallow the act of another's generosity, inhibiting them from an authentic expression of their own kindness. If we graciously accept the loving intentions of other people, a natural warmth of the human spirit glows in the hearts of both parties, satisfying both the need to give, and uplifting the receiver by way of the gift itself. When a gift is given with heart, and when the recipient shows true appreciation, it creates a thoughtful momentum that propagates human kindness beyond this exchange, the spirit of giving and receiving far greater than the gift itself could ever be.

201. A girl stubs her toe when she is off to the wrong adventure but then is set right

The pesky annoyance of a stubbed toe speaks to the higher self as the girl sets off on the wrong foot. While it is true that we can stub our toe even when we are on the right path, we will read such signs however our own inner conscience directs us in the language of our own wisdom. There is some irritating nudge that asks us wake up and face the present error, to reset the wrong adventure and make it right again. However large or small, some kind of reconsideration is necessary, our bearings need an adjustment. We examine what first comes to mind during this minor falter and listen to what arises in our own intuitive center as we determine what is wrong about our present adventure. With this inner guide, we can change course before the pains roughen up further along the way.

202. A pile of empty cocoons

A protective shell no longer needed is left behind. This pile indicates we are not alone in our voyage to freedom, there is a shared point of departure for these butterflies. Beautiful and natural, these cocoons were crucial to our early survival and our collective formative development was dependent on it. Having now outgrown this protective encasement, it is time to fly freely into a larger unknown world. We are permitted to explore whatever we wish, ready to fend for ourselves in all of life's glories and dangers. This glimpse back to our former nurturing homes makes certain our present transformation as we progress into a new cycle of advancement from our prior state of limitation. This newfound autonomy liberates us to discover the beautiful world, freed to proudly display the unique colors of our vibrant wings as we taste for the first time of wild nectars that call us.

203. Treasures are collected for a beloved elder

Honoring a beloved elder is one of the most well deserved demonstrations of respect. The elder has watched their youth turn into history, they've seen innumerable births and deaths, joys and sorrows. They have undergone changes and challenges in their inner and outer worlds to degrees unfathomable to those more youthful. They have loved and been loved, struggled and survived for more years than most, and thus have become a treasure trove of wisdom and story themselves. One way to appreciate the cherished elder is with a thoughtful curiosity of their lived experience, inviting them to share their favorite memories and speak their well-earned wisdoms. The moment calls to collect treasures for the respected elder, which might include something we lovingly made with our own hands or a special work created by a grandchild, or a presentation of gathered artifacts that have been meaningful to them in their own life, or a gift that comes with blessings for times to come. Whatever we give, this is a time to honor and respect the long life of the beloved elder.

204. A swamp dries up to receive fresh rain

The wetlands go dry to make space for a total renewal, sucked dry of moisture it is emptied completely. Following the evaporation of the old, waters are new again as fresh rain fills the space in this regenerative downpour that benefits the life of the entire swamp. Crystal clean water charges up the depleted environment, and quenched with vital life it flourishes again. Energies are exhilarated and we too are brought to life, revitalized as we drink in the essence of the falling rain. What had shriveled dry and turned stale is electrified by this shower, as a new reservoir of untapped potential settles in and fills the thirsty swamp.

205. Friends cut up photographs and rearrange them

This puzzling rearrangement feels a bit confusing, some kind of mixed up narrative is at play. The captured moments in the unaltered photographs have been severed from their original context, disassociating the mood of the initial snapshot. Of course this can be done for amusement or artistic effect in which case we must be clear of what new messaging the recrafted material perpetrates. Whether the result is art or chaos, we note the unreliability of accurate recollection of the past as it is, careful of how we preserve our memories and retrieve them later as lived truths. However we choose to play with the stories of our lives, the renditions of these narratives can become real in our minds even if we have incorrectly stored the memory of what actually happened. We consider how we reinforce the brief images that comprise our lived memories, what we revisit as visual keepsakes and photographs and what we think about when we see them, the storyboard of our own lives, the collection of stories we tell as our truths.

206. A man on a mountain sits still and breathes

A grand vista of perception on this mountaintop, quiet and still. The concentration is on the breath as we gaze across this expansive view, humbled by our smallness while also realizing how in tune we are with nature. When we begin to really observe the breath we develop a finer and finer focus that gradually becomes a meditational state. In this heightened state of awareness, a profound essence of cosmic consciousness fills us as we inhale the pristine air, and with the exhale we dissolve back into the universal everything. The rhythm and volume of our breath creates a quality of being that underlies the patterns of all we think, feel, and experience. On the summit we are calmed as we ride our spacious breath, our form nearly vanished as we become one with the mountains, one with the world, as much as we can in this moment of deep peace.

207. A tiger chases a rabbit

The tiger has the advantage of brute power and strength while the swift rabbit is cunning and agile. As we examine this wild pursuit, we can relate to each animal as a point of study in our own disposition. The tiger arouses our bestial warrior, the hungry nature of our primal selves who embarks on the chase with full force of body and will. The rabbit reminds us that those who appear inferior can outwit or trick their tracker to avert attack. As apex predator, the beautiful and powerful tiger is likely positioned for a favorable outcome in the natural order of the wild, so we accept this law of the jungle if the hunt is successful. In the way nature teaches us through life and death, such actions are part of the world and we honor the tiger's unparalleled potency, the awesomeness of such prowess and majesty. We also appreciate the survivability and perseverance of those smaller and more vulnerable. We may contemplate the possibilities of being on either side of such a heart-pounding chase, so would be wise to prepare for similar events through knowledge of our own unique combination of physical strengths, speeds, and wits that ensure our own survival.

208. A writer rips up her pages and starts over

A record of thought is abruptly destroyed, written pages suddenly ripped to shreds. This is a decisive gesture, free of defeat since the writer starts over in the same wave of momentum. There is a sobering realization that at some point our language failed to communicate the truth of what we wanted to convey. Whether the act was impulsive or carefully considered, the misaligned narrative is officially terminated and we immediately turn over a fresh page to begin again. We investigate which chronicles of our own telling have veered away from what we wish to express, and without pause we are more deliberate with precise language to accurately transmit what we truly want to say. It is important to correct trails of our personal messages that have misled, as one deceptive or deluded detour further scrambles what follows. Once the pages are torn there is no looking back, rather we clarify and move forward with the distortion cleared so we may better retell the tale.

209. A spider rolls up a wasp that is larger

The spider spins its own fibers for protection and shelter, its nearly invisible web woven to trap unsuspecting prey. The wasp is a relatively equal match for the spider who strategically spins its net where the wasp is known to fly, which gives an advantage to the wasp who then notices the spider that it will attempt to sting and paralyze. On the ground the outcome would be uncertain, but the determining factor here is that we are in the spider's domain, its well-built web has successfully captured the other predator. The silken encasement of the large prize rolling along the translucent web softens what could have been violently venomous and graphic with either side gnashing into the other with its toxic stinger or fangs. The home territory of the spider determined this adversarial defeat in an otherwise even match. We settle into the strange peace of this image thankful we were not struck with a more painful invasion, and understanding nature's ways we are encouraged by the spider, fed and secure in the structure of our own home.

210. A shaky hand holds a roll of keys searching for the one to fit the keyhole

The pressure is on in this apparent test as we shuffle through keys to see if we are allowed admission. We are granted the power of entry only if poised enough to find the correct key in time, a tenseness inherent in the situation as depicted by the shaky hand. Bravery, clear-thinking, and self-control must arise for us to function smoothly despite our anxiety. In order to open the locked door we must be swift and precise to effectively avoid the useless distractive keys to find the single one that unlocks access to this passage. This door is not easily opened for a reason, a great reward or sanctuary may wait behind it if we can settle our nerves, hold our head high and approach this challenge with the confidence that has gifted us with this opportunity in the first place. At the threshold of initiation we are worthy of crossing as long as we can identify the correct key, realizing once we pass we must maintain courage and strength to responsibly handle this privilege of access.

211. Moths glowing in the dark at night

A luminous night show is radiant and visible for those not sleeping, the moths so attracted to the light that they themselves are glowing, seemingly from within. The congregation of these incandescent wings touches us in the chilly darkness to seek flight towards the mystery of light, divinity, knowledge, some higher force that bathes us with its grace when we faithfully approach it. Enchantment enlivens the night, asking that we walk through the darkness and ponder these fluorescent illuminations as hints of truth

147

and intimations of secrets to which we normally fall blind. This night is not one for early sleep, active and alive it calls forth our imaginations and spiritual appetites, moving our own wings to fly straight into the bright light of great wonders. Tonight we saturate ourselves with this spiritual glow, and once we have our fill of the light we may then use this as fire for deeper inspiration and dreaming.

212. A thick layer of ice hardens the earth

This is a wintry season when growth ceases and we are left feeling cold and frozen. We might experience a hardening of our emotions and it could be difficult to connect with others due to the impenetrability of the thick ice. Rather than read doom in the message of this ice-capped earth, we remember that this energetic pause protects what lies beneath, future seeds that have yet to germinate. This condition allows us a necessary dormancy, challenging us to accept this stage where we have to generate a little more heat and feed the fire within, knowing we are not going to find it outside anytime soon. If we can move through this frozen period by stoking life inside and planning for what is to come, we will be ready to bring the awaiting vivacity to the surface when the season shifts. For now we blanket ourselves with the comfort of encouraging truths, knowing that states of matter must fluctuate for there to be any movement at all. As cold and lonely as the icy touch may currently feel, it is certain to melt, when we and all things are warm to the touch and blooming again.

213. A baby feeds from its mother for the last time

This intimate moment shares the bond between mother and child, an emotional occasion knowing this is the last time the baby will feed from the mother's body. As the expression of maternal nurture shifts into a new phase, the infant takes a significant step towards independence, ready to ingest food directly from the outside world. A natural cycle has ended, after the long gestation and post-natal nourishment there is no longer direct biological dependence on the mother. Her nutritive resources will fully return to her own sustenance and the child is prepared to consume for itself, each autonomous. As the mother knows, though this precious stage has passed, the energy and efforts it required are now freed to express love in another way. We celebrate the distinct wholeness of mother and child, and though the weaning might bring difficult emotions at first, we accept that the phases of life and love are ever in motion, always changing.

214. Trees fall horizontal in a windstorm

The mad winds roar strong in this stormy rage of weather. Chopped trees are falling, trunks knocked flat, an onslaught against the upright. This is a windstorm of power, gusts strong enough to level the trees, snapped to the ground by whirlwinds that throw us down alongside them in the spin, a pile of timber left behind. Placing ourselves parallel to the horizontal woodpile, we see the severed trunks correspond to our own overblown chaos fallen as detached thoughts. When our busy and scattered mentalities become too pressurized they blow frenzied as the winds, and in the way of the trees our own minds can fall flat when the force grows too strong. There will be a quiet calm at the end of the storm, a repurposing of the wood we can use for heat or building new structures, assembling new edifices of thought. The groves are open for plotting and replanting, and with a peaceful breath we blow a soft wind, fresh ideas stirring, new life coming. The horizontal trees leave their bones, supporting all to come.

215. A joyous and beautiful funeral

This end of life celebration beautifully honors the individual with good spirit and joy. As eventually all of our lives in these earthly bodies must come to a close, to have the fortune of departing through the energy of this festive spirit with our loved ones gathered around to smile and reminisce and escort the transitioning soul onward is a blessed way to pass. This crossing over ceremony invites us to respectfully peer into the spirit realm to send the departed on their way with blessings and positive energy so that they may peacefully move on while we keep a warm place for them alive in our hearts. We take this moment to celebrate those we have loved and lost, realizing that the true soul of the connection is never gone in the unchangeable way they forever touched us.

216. Women making cups and bowls on a riverbank

An immersion into pure femininity, this atmosphere flows with fertility and life. The movement of the vital river rolls by the women on the bank, imbuing them with its rejuvenating waters as they create.

The women themselves are receiving the natural forces of this living fountain as they carry the current forward to make cups and bowls as vessels of abundance to collect and share these life-giving waters. As they form the containers fit to receive this life, they exemplify the receptive feminine in her nurturing wisdom, much like the intuitive woman knowing when her own womb is ready to receive the impulse to conceive new life. There is a plentiful source of potent life force streaming by, so it is up to us to create the vessels needed to accommodate this bounty of life that pours forth. We are preparing for a new birth and at the headwaters we are ready, molding the receptacles from which fresh life will spring.

217. Crystal clear water in a bowl of pink granite on a mountaintop

We are raised to the pinnacle of purity in this perfect offering. The elements are pristine at these heights, crystal clean water kept energetically intact in a bowl of pink granite, its natural charge strengthened by the mineral. The highest praise is offered up with this presentation, a display worthy of divine consumption. We appreciate this majestic exhibition of harmonious stillness, a seamless perfection as a gift of beauty. It asks for nothing and requires no intervention, it is flawless as it is, stable and unmoving, untouched and unchanged by anything except by how time itself may change it. As we walk on holy ground, the mountain sanctuary asks us to maintain this quiet purity, keeping it clean as shown on this precious mantle of crystalline earth and water, inspiring us to treasure and care for all such places for the sacred beauty they hold.

218. Bats flying low to the ground in the evening

There is a sense of settling down into the evening even though the low-flying bats feel rather eerie. With the oncoming night the sky darkens, the bats descend, and in their blindness we may easily feel them brush past us like embodied shadows. We too begin to lose sight, and like the sonar communication of the bats, we are instructed to feel and sense our way through the nightfall. Hovering over the ground and outside the normal scope of vision an intuitive resonance guides us to where there is food or nourishment. Somewhat blind yet fully feeling, we take our perceptions with us we ascend with the low-flying bats when they rise again into nocturnal flight, sharing their visions beyond the eyes, those we ponder as we return with them to the inner depths of our own cave.

219. An army sharpens iron weapons

A tension is building, either a threat has moved an army to tune up their weapons for defense or there is something they are driven to fight for with offensive forces. A warlike suspense is gathering, as iron weapons promise a durable and potent attack once thrust forth. As the murmur of battle escalates with the sharpening of each weapon, we can prepare ourselves by refining our own protective assets and consider the occasions that would call for their use. We question if this hostile preparation is necessary at all, and if we do in fact have something truly worth fighting for, we must be able to clearly identify what it is. It is important to consider our allies and the integrity of our alignment with them, or lack thereof, and remain true to our strength of will and moral motivations. To obtain this clarity, self-knowledge and self-discipline are vital so that we do not get lost in unfounded aggression or confuse our purpose. Sharpened weapons point the way to our highest self so that we may avoid conflict when we can, yet also have the capacity to defend or assert ourselves when the inevitable wars of life, small and large, challenge us.

220. A crane lands by a bathing woman

This visitation from the sacred crane emphasizes the sanctity of the bathing woman. There is a meeting of earth and sky, the bird of graceful dance and longevity brings heaven to the naked body of the woman. Together this fusion embraces a holy moment where we may cleanse and energize ourselves. As the martial dance of the crane teaches us, the quality of our movement externally exhibits our inner vitality, most effective with a soft strength, neither overly forceful nor yielding, as is the way of water. When we come closer to this center, we align with the flow of the universe and its subtle undulations. If we bathe in this essence of purification and effort, naked and open to spiritual communication, the immortal parts of our spirit may be awakened, and with practice and refinement we work towards our destined bliss. The sacred waters cleanse our flesh and prepare us to fly like the crane and rise with enlightened strength in our own eternal flight.

221. Workers clear a cluttered road

A roadway has been blocked by some morass of accumulated junk. Useless materials carelessly littered over a route of access has hindered any opportunity for advancement. Despite this, we are now moving in a positive direction as workers are finally in the process of clearing the way. The removal of such chaos suggests we ourselves need to clean up our personal space to make room for something new. We have accrued too much, whether it is physical items clogging up our environment or mental storage wasted on holding useless information or entertaining too many distractions and memories. Whatever it is, we are in a mode of elimination and release, and it is imperative we remove the obstacles that block our progress. As we empty our clutter we feel lightened, making space for new inspiration as we open the road ahead so that without stumbling we may step onto the path that leads us to our next destination.

222. A spell worker learns how to become invisible

A higher degree of magical ability has been attained. Being a spell worker, this person is already on a supernatural path, though becoming invisible is a major universal power that reaches another level. This advancement comes with great responsibility, as once we enter dimensions beyond physical comprehension, we tap into energies that can become dangerous to us as neophytes. Meddling with energies beyond our mortal limitations takes us into vulnerable zones where no one protects us or even sees us but ourselves. Whatever new world we discover is teeming with countless other

154

entities, the good and malevolent alike, both certain to greet us at the gate. A state of invisibility suggests we are consciousness roaming outside of our bodily confines, meaning to some extent we have given up control of our physical form which then opens us up to other forces who may be capable of possessing our bodies and operations in the human earthly world. As long as we remain mindful and humble in our pursuit of mystical work and communication with formless existence, we can quietly explore these abilities and energies with care and benevolence.

223. A woman stares intently into a mirror

As the woman stares into her reflected face, her mirrored eyes show the woman her soul. With the self-awareness of this intent gaze, we are invited to take a deep look into our true nature, to study the strangeness of our own eyes. Whatever feelings arise as we stare reveal honest reflections of self-love or hidden deceit, what shines or wears heavy in our eyes. By observing ourselves this way, we gain a view of what others see as well, insight into the way we appear to the people in our life, influencing how they interact with us and interpret what we communicate. This moment invites a reflective revelation as we feel the thoughts behind our facial expressions, noticing the subtle glints of our eyes and what makes them spark, and if we are open and inviting or dissuasive and closed off, and most of all, whether or not our face that greets the world aligns with what we feel within and intend to express.

224. The full moon shines light on a celestial storm

The full moon as the greatest expression of the sun's reflected light shines forth upon a celestial storm. Energized first by the impulse of the sun's life-generating activity and illuminated further by the intuitive wisdom of the nurturing moon, the union of this clarified light creates a powerful awareness so that we may see the storm in its relevant light. Knowing that the orbit of the moon concentrates cosmic influences onto the earth, this revelation of light on the storm corresponds as well to the importance of balancing the solar and lunar energies in our own lives. If we can balance the decisive will to act, the solar, with the lunar patience to reflect on our emotional intuitions and move forward in this harmonious light, we can learn to ride both the beautiful and difficult celestial storms that inevitably befall us.

225. An altar of gemstones from all over the world

Gemstones as crystallized energy gathered from all over the world together create an altar of immense power. This image is full of great potential, exposing us to a vast assortment of raw earth energy, each gemstone with its unique crystalline vibration reverberating through its distinct geometrical shape. Such an array of gathered stones emits a massive cumulative resonance, an energetic powerhouse we can draw from and absorb into ourselves as subtle energies. With the present collection revered on this altar we have a chance to explore the properties of life-generating forces or shields of protection or any of the other myriad essences inherent in these diverse gemstones. We receive access to this magical platform where any conduit of energy we are seeking is sure to be found.

226. An ancient seed unlikely sprouts

The intrinsic timing of the seed has ripened, and along with the support of the present conditions of the environment, the sprout begins its life. Long dormant, the ancient seed took a long time to shoot, an unlikeliness that makes its eventual fruition all the more interesting. This could be a recovered strain of a long lost novelty, a forgotten heirloom, a reinstated treasure for the next generation. It might be something we ourselves have dropped and forgotten, a latent potential that required more time to pass before it could bear fruit. Whether the nature of the seed is clear to us or we need to till the soil and dig around for what we've missed, there is burgeoning life ready to break open from the surface. Though this ancient possibility seemed unlikely, we know that it is in fact ready to be born. This long-awaited moment tells us that now is the time, the circumstances are finally favorable to support the growth of this ancient seed.

227. A band playing beautiful music underwater

A sea of music is flowing under the surface, a full body of sound travelling through waves of water rather than air. We defy logic as we listen to the underwater band play beautiful music in this surreal and emotional place. In the depths of what lies beneath we are hidden and contained in this dreamy dissolution where we may fully release into the divine power of music. Immersed in this private world we are one with the hum of the watery womb, bathed in musical solace as the emotions of our deep visceral selves are touched. Held in these waters we dissolve into seas full of feeling, pure emotional nurturing and wholeness cradle us with the comfort of sonic lulls. Embraced by these soothing sounds we are tuned to the oceanic rhythms syncopated with all existence, ourselves moved deep inside the serene waves of this beautiful music.

228. Someone of long bad luck suddenly becomes lucky

A streak of misfortune has changed direction, a long bad trend suddenly takes a lucky turn. This is a message of restored hope, a reminder that even in the worst of times, no matter how unlucky we are or how relentless the bad force seems, a shift is always possible. In this case the good fortune comes suddenly, so whether this is a random lucky occurrence of sheer chance or it is the result of our personal effort to attract lucky situations, this is a pleasant surprise. This newfound luck gives us a chance to observe the choices and patterns of our actions, allowing us to piece together chains of energy that coincide with good luck and those that tend to clash with it. The further we refine these subtle observations the more we can turn the propensity for success into a habit by generating conditions in our lives for favorable energies to gravitate our way. At the same time we simply enjoy feeling lucky, grateful for the inexplicable blessings that shower down as divine grace.

229. A primitive medicine person sews wild stitches

We are in primitive circumstances. This is a traditional tribal role likely passed down over generations, directing us to the wisdom of ancestral roots as a solution to our present ailment. Something has been split open and whether it is a physical cut, a severed relationship, or some other strife that leaves us feeling torn, we are in need of a holistic remedy to reconnect what has broken apart. We look to healing wisdom of the medicine people, to ancestral knowledge so authentic that it lives on in their lineages as continuous proof. The miraculous effect of the primitive medicine worker combines their use of raw natural material with sincere spiritual invocation, where they themselves become an instrument of healing that can transfer the energy of these forces into the patient. This is a fundamental aspect to all traditions of natural healing, teaching us that simple cures backed by a spiritual source are most helpful to us now.

230. A community chants for its well-being

Many voices gather in this communal intonation, chanting as a group for their mutual well-being. The whole community exponentiates the effect of any one individual, and with such shared intent rhythmically pulsing as one, their effort is certain to impact the physical realm. As the practice of mantra shows us, established chants spread over numbers of people and years of time affirm and strengthen their frequencies, and they become actual structural vibrations that affect our dimension of reality. In this spirit we may identify what group in our own life needs an uplift of inspiration

159

whether it be our community at large, friends or family, or those with whom we work or worship, and we invite them to gather and chant or speak or pray with shared vocal passion for a common good.

231. A poacher gets turned on and killed by his own attack

An aggressor's attack has backfired, his poaching ambitions have turned on him resulting in his own death. The illicit trophy seeker has succumbed to hostile greed, defeated by a reversal of energy, ethically offensive strikes that boomerang back. Natural laws appear to come for retribution. We are clued in by this dramatic example to avoid such intense recoil, to consider the truth of our own downfalls before anything this serious consumes us. The motivating concepts that drive our activities create a self-replicating pattern that becomes the circuit of our lives. To stop a bad habit we must throw it out of the loop, which becomes harder the longer it is reinforced on the cyclic continuum. All of our actions together form our circle of experience, any part of which can return to us at any time, a notion that encourages us to correct anything we perpetuate that we do not wish to have backfire. The truth herein tells of our greatest punishments and our greatest rewards.

232. Wild animals graze on land where no humans have ever been

This untouched oasis is a reservoir of the wild world where nature self-sustains using its own sources of interdependent life forms and elements. The wild animals graze on plants sewn by their own seed, falling exactly as blown by the wind and carried by the insects. There are the right amount of animals to survive on what is provided, too few to deplete the vegetation but enough to consume what would otherwise grow to excess, creating a functional balance where all thrive. This natural haven establishes its own harmony, a time flow that carries all life into a state of equilibrium without any intrusion. We give pause to appreciate the act of non-doing, letting the natural way reveal its intrinsic knowing without our human tendency to manage and control. We hold sacred the natural wilderness, the bountiful land and the freedom of our untamed soul.

233. A tense cloud in the atmosphere breaks free

The vaporous gloom of this tight packed cloud has broken. Moisture bursts from the sky as the release of the pent up pressure in the atmosphere sets free our own emotional tensions. Anything we repress in the landscape of personal emotions can join the deluge, we let out a cry and let go whatever looms in our own dark clouds. As the downpour outside waters the earth, we too need a destination for our passionate outcry, and whether through sweat or tears, the suppressed heaviness must rush outward to alleviate the pressing force. An uninhibited creative flow is erupting from our most intense emotions, a cloud bursts open and gives way to the sun.

234. An earthquake creates a divide

The earth rumbles, the surface splits and cracks open a divide. This sudden rift puts us on one side or the other, a distinct dichotomy of place. Separated from the other half, we have lost access or influence with the other side, possibly even blocked from our home territory. We work to heal the divide and bridge the gap, and even if the physical chasm is permanent we strive for communication and cooperation with the other side. Reconciliation after such division is our present effort, to stabilize and adapt to the shaken ground so recently trembling under our feet. As we reestablish our footing we know the tremors of the earth can shake things up at any given time, so we stand firm yet cautious. Resolved to remain stable despite whatever may fall from under our feet, we have the resilience to integrate ourselves and the world around us, at peace with our unity as well as our separateness.

235. Footsteps crush vegetation but it springs up again

We see the supple strength of the vegetal world, the natural way it springs to the light, the optimistic way it stands tall, always bouncing back, defiant of gravity's downward hold but for the stable roots. When we reach to the light as is vegetation's way to rise and unfold towards the sun, we lighten ourselves and create space in our bodies with the zest for life pulling us up, while remaining grounded in the likeness of the plants' roots. As with the resilience shown in this botanical model, we too can bounce back up when we are crushed or feel beat down. With our head held high, our chest out proud, we stretch to the sky just as vegetation reaches high to the sun, upright and strong, unconquerable and not to be trampled. Nothing keeps us down here, no oppression can stop us, we always spring up again into the light, heavenward and growing.

236. A snake catches a mouse but then a hawk gets them both

In this predatory hierarchy, the snake exemplifies the ambivalence of all existence, the truth that everything alive consumes and will itself be consumed. The life cycle of the food chain and the devouring nature of time passing makes all bodies temporary. We are shown the snake as hunter who realizes sudden capture himself, all ranks transitory and relative as the mouse of prey has now the same status as the snake in the hawk's talons. The hawk flies away with a double feed for now, but as the message shows, we all end up vanishing into the same place of mysterious death. With the mouse we are humbled by our vulnerability as the snake consumes us, decisive and quick. We are reminded to avoid distraction or conceit, for the snake is then swept up by the hawk, who seeks what he finds with laser sharp focus. We all have our place in the hierarchy of life, so we savor our strengths and protect ourselves along the way, doing our very best to survive and find peace for as long as we are here.

237. A house of people are rapt by a charismatic speaker

An inspiring charisma has enraptured a crowd, an infectious spirit has charmed this house of people. This place and the allure of the speaker's message holds great influential power, a positive force that will set those in attendance on a better path forward. The beauty of the gathering is that each unique person is lit by the motivation and enthusiasm in a different way, and will in turn carry inspired understanding onward into their own lives from which the encouraging spirit will benefit more and more people. We are moved by the gift of oration and imagine the tone and dance of language, the cadence of the words spoken and the eyes sparkling with true inspiration, learning ourselves how to communicate our own passions we believe in so strongly.

238. A crystal ball splashes into water at the bottom of a well

Plunged into the depths, a crystal ball splashes down into the bottom of a well, driving a purifying energy through the waters. The entire container is vibrating with the crystalline buzz of the sphere. Settled into the basin of the emotional and feeling world, the resonance rings in the waters and all life it nourishes. Crystal balls can grant special sight to those who gaze into them, so as an image of the subconscious waters this opens an oracular view into our own personal depths as a private window through which we can access our authentic inner guide as our truest source of instinctual knowing. As we imagine this crystal ball inside of ourselves to contain everything, our entire well of identity and feeling, the seer who sees from our deepest sense of self, we can feel its smooth spherical form settle into the foundational base of our being. With this we have a solid reserve of guidance and clarity that we may tap into anytime, our resonant waters in tune with the sacred jewel within.

239. A young hero is anointed

This young hero has been chosen, set apart from the common order to accomplish a special task. Anointed with divine power, the consecrated hero is now an instrument of the heavens, selected to complete an honorable mission. The absorption of the ritualized oil is the pouring in of spirit as aid and protector, enabling a godlike support to empower and work through the receiver. This calling is beyond ordinary magnitude, inspiring us to recognize and anoint the hero in ourselves as well as the heroes of our era, in our personal lives and the greater world. Here we begin a great quest backed by higher powers entrusting us with their strength and attention. Our bravery is recognized, our distinguished abilities have been acknowledged, and our purpose revealed. As an auxiliary to a higher will providing us access to powers greater than our own, we believe in ourselves and hold faith as we step forth on the hero's journey that calls us.

240. A group of gamblers shuffle cards

The tables are cleared and the game starts over, the elements of possibility with various outcomes shuffled once again. At this new beginning we have the opportunity to strategize based on our previous gains and losses and rethink our approach. Observing this game of chance we can look beyond the gamblers and see that all aspects of life are constantly shuffled into random order, surprising cards are pulled and we are dealt hands often outside our control. The nature of the game however, is the freedom we have in how we choose to play it, the ability to improve our strategy and pick up a few tricks along the way. We are wise to learn from our mistakes, knowing when to show our cards, when to hide them, when to raise our gambled assets, and when to fold. During this determinate shuffling, a new order is created for the next round of events. We are ready to play this game of fixed circumstances with skill and insight, sure to study the people with whom we engage, and to consider our most balanced strategy for whatever calls us to the table.

241. A volcano erupts and static electricity runs rampant

This fiery burst is electric and alive, hot currents thrashing and flailing everywhere, birthed from the boiling magma of the underworld. Pressurized chambers beneath the surface are breaking open, an active eruption of flowing molten lava is exploding outward. We are dealing with volatile flares of static electricity, whips of lightning strike the atmosphere, chaotic collisions ready to transfer matter from one state to another. An immense surge that was swelling beneath the earth is no longer able to subdue this built-up energy as massive voltages rupture the space. In the eye of this electric maelstrom, we work to control our own charge by opening ourselves as conductors for the energies we do wish to receive and isolating ourselves from those we do not. We give this immediate focus, as the volcano is erupting now and the static vapor on the magma is hot!

242. A fisherman's net captures a school of fish

A school of fish visually indicates a plentiful population, and the fisherman and his net suggest a healthy local catch, the consumption of clean food being an essential part of human harmony with the natural world. The fresh fish provides a taste of pristine health obtained through the purity of the gentle net to bring in naturally sourced food with the efforts of the fisherman's hands as an unpolluted process. We must participate and consume within this natural cycle to avoid the artificial alternatives that throw the entire living cycle out of balance. The living world is interrelated, all beings eat of it and then feed it with their own bodies and the substances they excrete, bringing the endless cycle around once more, becoming food to us again. Within this universal harmony we strive to sustain ourselves from nature's sources as directly as possible. Here we are invited to do so purely as we appreciate the healthy abundance we are offered in this clean catch.

243. Igloos melt at the fire breath of a dragon

The insulated homes of the frozen arctic have melted in the flame of the dragon's fire. Its blazing breath has left us out in the cold hard open, unsheltered and challenged to overcome this obstacle. The winged beast as foe can petrify the quivering mortal yet as a mystical ally it bestows magnificent empowerment, so in the single purge of this exhale we must choose. Does exposure to otherworldly change and the aftermath of the unknown cripple us into a fear that will leave us freezing without a home, incinerated ourselves by the encounter with the mystical monster we cannot believe and therefore never defeat? Or rather do we embrace its thundering wings by conquering the moment, by roaring back with courage and staring the dragon in the eye as a source and measure of our own strength. In our victory, we rebuild our homes enhanced with new vision and gain a greater appreciation for the comfort it provides, and most of all we walk away with our head held high and our spirit unbroken.

244. A woman finds shelter from a hailstorm underground

This battering storm falls as chunks of pounding ice. Physically and emotionally distressed the woman is in need of shelter. She finds refuge underground, a protective descent into the underworld to safely wait until the storm passes. Heavier implications may arise with the energy of this hammering storm, so it is noteworthy that the self-reliant woman finds the sanctuary herself. She needs no hero, asks for no savior, but by necessity she successfully finds the passage to her asylum. While we remember that storms always pass, there is nevertheless violence raging outside and we have full permission to retreat in a comfortable abode of our own selection where we feel secure to ride out this clobbering downpour. In this moment a safe harbor is needed to preserve our energy and rejuvenate for the clearer skies sure to come tomorrow.

245. A tribe climbs trees to harvest acorns

Climbing trees to harvest the many acorns with cooperative effort is a scene of growth and ascent, a harvest of power. The prowess of the tribe and the majesty of the grand oak are connected by the acorn, humans being one of many creatures that eat the tiny fruit, packed with such nutritive vital force that it houses the latent power to become a fully mature oak tree. Further efforts are requisite to obtain true life force as we see in the preparation of the acorn, from climbing the trees and collecting them, to grinding them as finely as possible before the multiple long soaks and rinses needed to effectively leech away the tannins. The tribal bonding, the willingness to work hard, and the gratification of eating from the oak as one of

168

the largest and most potent life forms on earth, teaches us that the greatest rewards are found hidden in the simplicity of collective effort. If we wish ourselves to be strong and vital, work is required to reap the strong and vital superior harvest.

246. A tricked man is chained out of his own house

A trickster is afoot, this man chained out of his own house warns us to open our eyes and remain clear. At this time we must think twice before revealing anything sensitive or making serious agreements with anyone, as the current moment necessitates caution. We maintain confidence when we speak and listen, when we walk, and as we interact with others in any way, deterring any display of vulnerability or naiveite that would attract swindlers and cheats. The chained out man insists by example that we avoid tying ourselves up with a bad deal, to evade gullibility and sufficiently contemplate anything suspicious presented to us at this time, especially in regards to our home and our freedom. We can relax our guard a little more as we understand the lesson, and whether we need this as only a brief consideration or more broadly applied into our lives, it is vital to outsmart the trickster with discernment and a focused mind.

247. The scales of an injured reptile shimmer iridescence in the sun

A shimmer of hope gleams over the scales of the injured reptile, the sun's rays reflecting a special quality of light that somehow promises to heal. Despite the injury, an iridescent rainbow shines with a luminous magic, highlighting such miracles as the regenerative abilities of reptiles. There is a lustrous beauty in this flicker of light where the stoic reptile basks in the restorative sun as its remedial powers begin their work. With this optimistic emphasis we enhance our own curative capacities, positivity and joy always conducive to the healing process. No matter the injury, whatever damage or grievances we must overcome, we are regenerated by this therapeutic light. As the scales of the injured reptile flash their colorful iridescence, we too emanate our radiant revival, the healing reflection of the sun's light bouncing from us back into the world.

248. Two magnets inch together from opposite ends of the earth

Such attraction from opposite ends of the earth is significantly intense yet slow, as the two magnets are only inching closer together. The power of the pull that longs for connection from so far away creates a suspense, we might desire the magnets move faster. Despite our anticipation we are nonetheless patient knowing that a genuine magnetic field gravitates as it must. The object of our attraction is detected and the incredibly strong magnet pulls us in, and though the actual full connection is prolonged, this interim of unhurried exploration will make the arrival all the more gratifying. Inching closer to their synergistic completion, these perfect opposites have turned towards each other, certain but unrushed to complete themselves with the other half that makes them whole.

249. An owl leads home a lost child

The wandering child was lost, vulnerable, and alone, susceptible to all sorts of encounters marauding in this wilderness of the owl. As the onlooker we fear for the naïve child stepping into the darkness, where dangers wait at every turn, the spirit of the lost child likely to be abducted in the night. This situation calls for us to return to our own inner child and become the inquisitive innocent, abandoning all security to travel through our fears and into the unknown. We lose ourselves by necessity into this dark night of the soul, wandering the loneliness until we feel helpless. As messenger of darkness, the realms of death and dream, it is the owl who escorts us from the wilderness when it is time, and spared calamity, we are deepened with a new knowing. Where we were lost, we have now been found, and on wings of wisdom we are guided home again.

250. A naïve youth resists seduction

A sense of self-control in the tempted youth exhibits an early mark of virtuous character and promise. Showing this level of restraint before the harsh experiences of mistakes have time to mature into integrated lessons proves an inherent clarity in the individual, a high aptitude for self-discipline and willpower. We are clear that the message is not to reject pleasure itself, only the false enticements that turn out to be foolish and of poor choice in the end. If we are discerning we can distinguish seductions that drain or harm us, while accepting the honest pleasures of true satisfaction, as the restrictions of an overbearing morality can cancel good opportunities, a backlash that becomes its own naïve mistake. However difficult it

171

may be to discriminate or resist temptations, we work to only open ourselves to authentic fulfillments that truly serve us, ones that give us honest love and move us forward on our highest personal paths.

251. A villain shakes bottles of bubbling poison

Shaking and bubbling in the villain's hands, this toxin is active and ready for immediate administration. Something antagonistic is underway, so we must be ultra-aware of what we ingest by substance and word alike, knowing poison can come in many guises. The toxicity of the brew could be obvious, intense enough at first taste that we know to spit it out, or else it could appear innocuous, disguised, and therefore our most acute observations must detect the hidden poison. Whether or not we are in direct interaction with the villain, we must face the truth that deadly concoctions do exist and what we take into our bodies, minds, and spirits can be medicine or poison. We keep a watchful eye and pay attention to all we consume, and with this we convert the poisonous intent into its opposite quality of detoxification and renewal, a transcendence that inverts the death trap, a new life quality that becomes the villain's defeat.

252. Tangled copper wires clutter a space

Copper wires conduct electric information so this tangled mess indicates cluttered communication. These jumbled wires are signaling crossed messages, meaningful content scrambled up and inaccessible in the disorder. To clear up the lines, we must unravel the wires and eliminate distractions that are mangling up the transmissions we are meant to receive. As we untangle the confusion we sort the relevant messages out of the clutter so that we do not mix-up the new arrangement. The pliability of copper gives us a generous flexibility to shape our lines of communication as we intend them to be understood, a renewed space stripped of all misunderstandings. After we learn to recognize kinked up wires and correct the twists and tangles along the way, we prevent accumulated misconceptions that obscure accuracies. From this point forward we are articulate and effective in what we transmit, cleared to express anything with full coherence.

253. A mist suspends life in midair

This is a freeze frame of a gentle mist, a display of life harnessed in midair, an exhibition of glorious life. The finest perceivable droplets hover as a soothing vapor where this ephemeral consciousness tranquilly floats over us. A pure stillness saturates us as we pause from all animation, immersed into this strange mist that washes away the temporal and gives a brief glimpse into the timeless now. Hydrated with pure life we bathe in this supra-sensory moment. In this fleeting instant we feel forever quenched, absorbing this gift as a positive impression in our soul, the more of which we can collect, the more we become and emanate such subtle life forces. As we let this imprint soak in, we are refreshed and focused on the present now, paused to enjoy the airborne life we may otherwise mistake as empty air, rather than know it as ether abundant.

254. Skeletons dance around in secret when no one is looking

This dance of the living dead celebrates a secret passage where two worlds are bridged together. The foundational skeletons are shaken loose of their flesh as a worldly bond and are free to roam in the realm of spirit. We examine the spiritual essence that moves our deepest selves to dance and express ourselves when no one is looking, what remains when we are stripped to the bone. As we spin the excitement of this ethereal self into motion, learning to sense ourselves beyond only form, we realize the lively existence of invisible entities of all kinds as they too are dancing around when we are not watching. These skeletons give us a view into their private dance, inspiring us to shake up our own inner structures to reveal the secret spirits we celebrate deep inside of our own bones.

255. A dead beast is skinned for leather

We cringe at the mention of a dead beast, so we may transfer this repulsion into an ethical focus that ensures we treat the fallen animal with respect. When such a dreadful yet natural image of death befalls us we must do the best we can with what the situation leaves us, approaching all death with reverence. A resourceful human society obtains their materials for needed goods from natural sources with organic processing, so using this hide for leather is harmonious with nature while also preventing the support of alternative synthetic products that pollute the earth from production to disposal. We consider the greater processes behind what we buy and consume, appreciating the life and energy that have generated the provisions that allow us to thrive.

256. A starved woman ravages smoked meat from a bone

A long desperate hunger has found delicious relief and this woman gladly sucks it down to the bone with no shame. She ravages the smoked meat in utter satisfaction, slurping the savory juices in full surrender to the joy of this satiation. After suffering starvation this indulgence is well-deserved, a fulfillment to be enjoyed to the fullest. The woman is not developing a hedonistic habit per say, but rather she is totally released in the pleasure of the moment, enraptured in the substance and flavor of this gratification. There is no holding back in this permissive flash, a special time is allotted to loosen restraint and treat ourselves, the last gristle of meat happily devoured.

257. An abandoned baby is found crying in a carriage

The newborn is crying to be heard, abandoned in its carriage the baby is in immediate need of attention. This situation calls for abrupt rescue. Whether this is an actual child or the infancy of some other creation or responsibility, this new life is dependent on its creator or another caretaker to guide it. Thankfully, the infant is saved by this timely response, and found in its carriage a small sense of comfort remains. Either returned home or adopted, the baby appears to have found safety and is headed to its new place of support where the undeveloped work, the barely started project, the baby child, the neglected task, is again ready to be nurtured and developed. Whatever it is, something or someone has been abandoned and left crying for nourishment and love, asking us to listen and reclaim responsibility for this precious life nearly forgotten.

258. A self-loving woman adorns herself with butter and wax

We feel the radiance of this woman, the emanation of warmth and beauty beaming from the rich moisture of her skin. She shines with a healthy glow and as we imagine the balmy butter spread along her body we are prompted to emulate this luxurious adornment. When we treat our body to self-care rituals we bathe ourselves with wellness, a deep imprint of love and nurture that enhances our health and beauty, maximizing the performance and longevity of our one and only physical vehicle in this life. The skin as the entirety of our external sheath, our protective shield, is a huge spread of sensory perception, the interpretive receptor that conveys to our mind the content and impressions of our experience. We stimulate a deep healing as we massage these beneficial elixirs into our skin with our own loving hands as we engrain profound love and acceptance for ourselves.

259. Two different plants cross-pollinate into something new

The cumulative effect of reproduction over time is a staggering thought to ponder, both genetically and in regard to the proliferation of ideas. When two distinct beings procreate something beyond themselves to which they each contribute, the combined third is born into its own independence that despite its sovereignty continues to represent a part of each of its progenitors. These parents, in this case the two plants, are also themselves the product of two separate entities, such a thought evoking the complexities of limitless diversity that make reproductive life fascinating. It is clear in this picture that the offspring from this pollination is of a wholly different kind of plant than either parent, so this is the introduction of a new specie, or a new idea, altogether. Whether of thought or partnership or plant, the generative energies at play are drawing two different but complementary lineage strains together to create something truly groundbreaking, unlike anything ever known before.

260. An enormous pendulum is hypnotizing its watchers

The sway of this enormous pendulum is heavy and hypnotic, inducing a lull that sends its spectators into a trance. We surrender our mental activity to observe this swing of time, a gravitational magnetic that pulls us into its steady rhythm as we release into this pulsation. When we relax our mind and shut down the distractions of analytical thought we are able to bypass the critical factors of our conscious mind and elicit unconscious insight. As we focus our gaze upon this stable swing, we eliminate the need to entertain disruptive thoughts which allows us to settle into a neutral state of mind. With our visual attention fixated on the motion of the pendulum, we evade our normal habitual mental fluctuations and are opened to access our subconscious selves where hidden and suppressed feelings and qualities of self can be revealed, the magical boon of the hypnotic.

261. Clothes worn in battle are washed and whipped dry in the wind

The blood and sweat of battle is washed clean, the fight is over. The stench of hatred has flowed away in cleansing waters, any linger of filth beat dry by the wind. A solemn echo of the battle seems audible in the whips of these worn clothes, and though renewed it is as if the ghosts of the fallen breeze by and momentarily inhabit them, the slaps of the fabric crying for all that was fought for and lost. For the victorious, the garments are enlivened by wind, waving like flags as we sit back with relief proud of how we fought for our cause. This post-battle renewal shows the evaporation of the peril and strife of the conflict. The clothes are washed clean, and as we wait for the wind and sun to fry off the remaining hostile energy down to the last drop, we stay quiet and let our own adversarial energies fade away. Then all calms down and there is only peace.

262. Plagues of locust come for the grain but for the first time men storm them away

Swarms of locusts come to devastate the grain, but thankfully they are defeated, stormed away by these men for the first time. The triumphant standoff against this plague of destruction potentially breaks the trend of decimation for some time to come, as long as we learn and remember to apply the strategy of our success in the future. In this image lies the essence of all our victories, the locust plague as a wrathful confrontation that challenges us to stand tall in gales of retribution. When voracious invaders taunt our labors and conspire to steal our fruits, we must have the stamina and courage to chase the horde out of the fields. Where we have sown our hard work and loving effort, we prevail over our enemies no matter how strong the swarm.

263. A man dodges a fatal sword strike by inches

The man has dodged the strike of the sword, the deadly blade has sliced right past him. We note this is not on account of the swordsman's error but on our ability to avoid the attack. Ensured we will walk away unscathed, we understand even so that we must dynamically evade this startlingly narrow close cut, and thus remain vigilant. The practice of concentration on our surroundings is the important power here, and in ways big and small it develops a cognizance that enables us to turn away from the swing of such blows. Awareness of our bodies within the space we are moving makes us kinetically fluent and mentally responsive so that we walk through the world equipped with indisputable confidence that protects us. We aim for seamless strides that empower us to hollow out the line of attack and dodge these fatal strikes.

264. Dead souls cross the veil and come to life for a day

A day where the dead are remembered, if not fully incarnate as they cross the veil and visit amongst us. The imagination of today inspires a remembrance of souls we love who have died, a resurrection of their spirit through story or in whatever way honors them best. The festive day blurs the veils and we feel free to interact with anyone as an immortal soul, an eternal imprint always alive in our hearts. We entertain the presence of the deceased and imagine indulging them in the worldly pleasures we still enjoy, laughing and partying with us. We feel their spirits inhabit our realm and welcome them with offerings and respect. Even the walking bodies still biologically alive who seem to carry dead weight can be reanimated

179

today in this revival. Any being from any part of time receives a flash of recognition as we all join in this immortal celebration, perhaps separated by body but all together in the spirit of now.

265. A sorcerer dreams of a tiger claw and really finds it

When we visualize an outcome with a focused clarity, or transpose a dream into worldly ambition, we begin to create the conditions within ourselves that allow it to manifest on the material plane. Our thoughts and conceptions roll into behaviors and ideals which determine the energetic unfolding of events around us and what we have conditioned ourselves to notice is what we will find. This is the task of the sorcerer, who works towards perfecting this process to orchestrate a reality of their choosing. A tiger claw is a totem of power, one that this particular sorcerer is granted through dream consecration, linking their imaginative power to earthly reality. We seek the strength of the tiger to pursue our own talisman, our emblem of power, the spark of dream delivering the expectant manifestation.

266. A sharp fanged beast breaks up a crowd

Teeth are barred and the fangs are sharp, a display of authoritative power that gives the beast full control over the group. Whether this monstrous interference is to stop a greater problem from occurring within the mass of people or it is the threat of the creature itself that is the terror, we are sure to run with the crowd as a natural and appropriate reaction, unless we are meant to face the beast. Once we have escaped the panicked atmosphere we can ponder the nature of the beast, considering the lens through which we judge our situations and the filters that provoke our fears. We reflect on the possibility of a misguided reaction to the sharp-fanged beast, as of course the appearance of deadly fangs does not necessarily mean they are out to eat us. We consider the point of stress that forces us to flee and whether we are doing so on our own behalf or blindly following a herd mentality without taking a deeper look.

267. The only humans with stones as eyes find one another

Distinctly unique humans find one another, the only ones with stones as eyes upon which they may now mutually gaze in the special way these two are alone capable. This is a soulmate connection with the absolute destined partner, the single one in existence who can truly appreciate this outstanding and peculiar shared quality that otherwise makes us feel lonely or misunderstood. Such a visceral comprehension of another person in this reciprocal way deeply unites the individuals in a place where true love can arise through this reflective recognition, where we meet the beloved as the perfect other who shares our most unique characteristic in a common bond that strengthens the relationship beyond anyone else's understanding, surpassing even our own wildest dreams.

268. A mangled path is cleared of debris

This garbled path blocked the way, obscuring the journey and confusing the destination. Progress had been impossible and inspiration was distorted for anyone called to this route of exploration. An entire vein of knowledge or culture, practice or training, some avenue of thought or experience had at least challenged travelers to access, if not closed the entrance altogether. However, the path is freshly cleared of debris and available now for discovery, and whether we embark on the trail alone or with fellow seekers, this is a call to step onto this open track, now free of the hazards that once choked our way. We pace ourselves for a smooth advancement as we approach this new opportunity, wide open and waiting for us to take the next step.

269. Two women read tea leaves together

The communion of two women opens a channel of double intuition, a dual receptivity that refines the interpretation of the infusion. The tea plant informs with the deva of its own essence, an ancient source of prophecy as the leaves lay steeped and settled in their oracular placement. Suffused by the water, the tea carries the emotional aptitude to read the foretelling message to the mediums who drink it. The magic of tea is that we can ingest it while viewing the source of what we sip before our very eyes, we drink in what also remains external at the same time. This is the jewel of the practice, observing the delicate impressions left behind from what we have taken within, awakening a portal to divine messages. Along with these insightful women, we synchronize the outer with the inner, appreciating the leaves of our ceremonial tea as an artful means of guiding us to our own true oracle.

270. A dedicated one masters their art

Mastering an art requires steady effort to develop a skill or quality with unwavering commitment and continuous practice over a long period of time. With such uninterrupted dedication and patience we acquire and build upon specific skills, developing finesse to forever refine and perfect our form on this gradual ascent towards mastery. As long as we are earnest and remain focused, undeterred in the face of distraction and tenacious to plow past plateaus, the highest expressions of our chosen path promise to reach into the levels of mastery. Devotion is the insignia of the message, as nothing of true mastery comes quick or easy. We set our sights on a goal that empowers us, an art or a practice of self-development, or work in the name of a noble cause, and fully committed to excellence of the craft, we dedicate ourselves completely to its regular practice. As we advance our skills of the art itself, we begin to experience a full energetic ascent as an ongoing evolution that extends into every aspect of our lives. With mastery of the art comes mastery of the self.

271. A healer grinds spices and barks with a mortar and pestle

This is raw natural healing at its best, spices and barks as wild grown medicines, ground by the stone of mortar and pestle with the power of our own hands. The energy behind this production is entirely organic, generated by conscious life born of the sun, unaltered by manmade electricity or mechanical processing, free of additives. As the spices and barks are ground with the rhythmic motion and pressure of the healer, a rapport is engaged between the person and the energetic properties of the plant. When the aromas and volatile oils of the plants are released, the preparation is enlivened and accessible to the healer as a workable medicine. The way of our present healing is to open ourselves to raw vital energies around us, deriving our therapeutics as much as we can from the natural world, keeping the organic circuit of genuine energy as pure as possible by remaining close to nature and the sincere work of our own two hands.

272. Two ancient warring families make peace

A long time grudge is finally forgiven, a quelled hatred has restored peace. The two families have been warring for so long that their grounds for opposition have lost relevance. Rivalry nullified, a truce has been settled as they lay down their weapons. When we inherit contention over generations of prejudice or combat, it loses justification over time, if it had any to begin with at all. Ignorant resentment and outdated loathing need reassessment in this time of amity. Everywhere possible we must surrender our abhorrence and forgive the war, for the peace of our entire family and a whole other family as well, depends on this treaty of long due resolution that will benefit many more lives to come.

273. A stampede suddenly breaks from pure silence

Something unexpected has shattered the silence, startling a group to rush away in a stampede of panic. Everyone is on their feet, barging forward in a frenzy to escape from whatever brash noise triggered the fury. The sudden break from pure quiet is shocking, the disorderly force transferred into the charge of the masses, and with the power of numbers this stampede is able to plow over and smother almost anything. The dramatic uproar has created a communal raucous, fear driving the assembly forward, most of them blind enough to follow the frontliners straight off a cliff if that is where they are led. After this intense surprise shoots us to our feet, we either deal with the disruptive shift with strength and endure with the group if we indeed face an actual threat, or we realize the false alarm and with caution we remain untrampled as we suavely step aside and let the misguided pandemonium pass by.

274. A crackling fire spits sparks

This crackling fire is vocal, volatile, little spits of it lashing out to be seen. Mesmerized by the whips of talking flames we are wide-eyed, gazing in awe while at the same time alert, careful to avoid the burn of an errant spark. If we are fully present, we can absorb the electricity of this etheric heat burning alongside us, its vibrant pops stoking our own internal fires that enflame our passions, the furnace within that fuels all of our vital processes and inspirations alike. Just as we have no earthly life without the sun, so too do we need the terrestrial counterpart of its solar rays, heat as fire that can burn steady or combust with action-packed flares as do these wayward

185

sparks. Condensed vital blasts are shooting out within our reach, energy available to us if we communicate with the mystery and fully release into the language of the fire.

275. The wind changes direction quickly many times

Messages are muddled, information is whirled around and our direction is unclear. Forthcoming times might feel more unpredictable than usual, and we are likely to erratically change our mind as we strive to find our way forward. As the wind swirls everything around in varying directions, our focus is obfuscated and we are dizzied with no bearings. These unstable gusts scramble communication, transporting thoughts and perceptions into a whirlwind of confusion possibly leaving us uncertain of even our most basic understandings. It is difficult to hold onto anything at this time so we must be patient with these fluctuations, challenged to pinpoint the convergence where everything blown around will meet when the wind calms down. If we find a center point of stillness amid these vacillations, we stay balanced to withstand the flustered forces, which ironically then become our great equalizer.

276. A huge glass bottle fit for a giant is dug up in the sand

A giant glass bottle excavated from the sand is a substantial discovery, an opportunity to shake hands with the great size of another time. The enlarged girth teaches our palms to spread and our fingers to extend wide, a giant stretch to hold the giant jug, an act that itself promotes growth. If the rest of our body follows, we will stand higher and prouder, our lungs will expand so that we are more oxygenated, enriching our blood which pumps up our brain and enlivens our extremities, and we become smarter, happier, healthier, and more motivated. We have dug up our voluminous treasure, we have pulled magnificent glass from the sand, and touched by its colossal power this bottle offers us a giant gulp of its humongous potential.

277. Tiny footprints found in deep dark caves

We tour the deep dark caves of the tiny, examining the underground footprints in this abyss of the otherwise untrodden. This descent into our private world asks us to observe the bedrock of our character, what is etched into its structure, the memories and deep impressions collected over our lifetime. We have found traces of experience that offer attention, fragments that have broken off or are chiseled with story, anything that hides inside our deep dark caves now invites us to look. These tiny prowling entities are among the components that make up our unified self, living inside our core as the underlying stratum within that continuously informs us of our own inner nature. We tread in the place where no light is shed to view the dark details of what has gradually conglomerated over time. If we choose we may step in and adjust the footpaths for a new subconscious perspective.

278. Determined scribes hurriedly scribbling

The muse is abundant, the wisdom is pouring, the expression of words is transmitted to these scribes nonstop as their pens are flowing. This copious revelation is rich with inspiration, articulations are streaming by that need to be captured. We must be sharp, quick to comprehend all that is coming at us, to write down everything we can as we try to understand and intelligently apply the content as well as possible. Scribes have the important task of clearly converting thoughts to words so that others can receive the concepts and learn from them. When we are concise with our ideas they can evolve into further ideas, linking complex thoughts together to make them relative and applicable and therefore useful. This is a time of rapid communication and learning, a time to stimulate and honor our need for knowledge and literary intellect, open to receive and transcribe our own dictations as inspired.

279. A small child covers an elder with a blanket

As the beginning and end of a circle meet at the same point, and as the new moon is the merger of waxing and waning, humanity is this way with the young child and the elder. Though on opposite sides of the cusp, the very young and very old are closer to the gate of life's passage than the middle majority. It is here the most important traits of humanity are most illuminated, natural needs such as the empathizing comfort shared in this caregiving act of the small child. Each less concerned with worldly affairs than any other life phase, the child just beginning their story and the elder having completed most of theirs, they are less distracted than the average person caught in the busyness of career and relationship complexities. As the elder relaxes under the warmth of the blanket, we feel the purity of an authentic loving gesture from the human heart, most tender and true in the young child and the seasoned elder. Let them inspire us to comfort and be comforted by those around us for the pure human joy of giving and receiving love.

280. Rich syrup is squeezed from leaves of a tree

This great reward is ripe for harvest, syrupy abundance is seeping from the leaves. We can taste the sweetness, we want to lick it off our fingers as the elixir pours forth. It is time to reap the sugary prize, thick and oozing, ready to be squeezed, a patient fruition from seed to sap. With such vital extract running from these leaves of plenty, we know the tree itself must have been well fed and consistently nurtured. It is time to savor the sweet treat so generously provided, remembering to again feed the tree to perpetuate the ongoing cycle of exchange with nature as the driving force of all life. This reciprocation is an ideal that raises the quality of all things, and having tasted of what is delicious, we then care for the tree so that we may taste of it again. As well as we love her, she continues to provide. May the mutual love always be so generously sweet.

281. A man and a woman hang upside down together

The man and woman are turned upside down, a complete reversal of all viewpoints, an inversion of gravity. This affects not only their visual processing but also their hormones and bodily functions, and, psychologically there is quite possibly an overturn of emotion, perhaps what landed them here to begin with. However scary or uncomfortable it might be at first, hanging upside down decompresses the spine while alleviating body tension and bad moods. The man and woman are improving themselves as they hang together on this moment, after which a common new outlook is assured. When they are upright again they will proceed lighter on their feet, moving forward harmoniously with a newfound clarity and a refreshed perspective.

282. A treasured vase breaks into a thousand jewels

A glimpse of impermanence, this smashed vase reminds us that everything is temporary. We might be reactive and upset at first, but then we see that our broken treasure has transformed into a thousand jewels. As we consider the transient nature of all things we ask ourselves what we truly value, and when we are able to isolate the qualities that determine our sense of worth we can extract and preserve the essence of our treasures when the physical forms inevitably break down. We can apply this concept to all of life, knowing that whatever shatters before our very eyes, no matter how hard the loss, at whatever speed it all comes crashing down, with a deeper look, we can transform any broken treasure into a thousand jewels, the cherished essence preserved, yet now repurposed with a new direction and a broader reach.

283. Meager grains are pounded to relieve famine

During this challenging time, extra work is required to provide basic needs on a large scale. Mutually hungry and in need of nourishment, we must pull together with others to conserve efforts and pool resources to ease suffering. As we streamline our exertions to maximize efficiency, we become more resilient and adaptable as we learn to get by on less. This forced frugality teaches us to appreciate all we have and that nothing in life is ever guaranteed. With perseverance we hold faith that our troubles will pass, maintaining the attitude that after the harshest difficulties we experience the greatest relief, and the image confirms that the famine is in fact relieved. Knowing this, we might gain perspective that our situation could be much worse and perhaps we experience overwhelming gratitude that though there are only meager grains that must be pounded, there is still food on the table.

284. Hard ground is broken up to receive life

The surface has been compressed, trodden over time and hardened into lifeless ground. As this inert earth hosts no life, we in the same way are unable to conceive inspiration if we are packed down too tight, as without inner space beneath the surface we have no room for roots to spread or air to flow, for ideas and designs to incubate and then flourish. The time however, has come, the compacted ground is finally tilled, aerating the depths and tenderizing the surface, awakening the promise of new life. Reinspired and uplifted, this cultivated space is ventilated and open, ready to receive sprawling roots for fruitful growth. No longer stomped on or suffocated, trampled and dry no more, we are spacious and receptive, flattened hopes turned over into jovial mounds reaching for new light, fertile and ready to rise.

285. A crystal on a crystal on a crystal that grows every direction

The multi-dimensional lattices that formulate the crystalline structure are conductors that can amplify, transform, or repel energies. This crystal has formed another crystal which has yet produced another, an exponential rise to the third power and still growing, an ongoing amalgamation extending into a great reach of influence. As this broadening vortex of energy expands, we see that to an increasing degree its power spreads, such as in the way a demonstration of kindness touches another and then they are kind to someone else in turn making the next one kinder and so on. The entire matrix of the universe operates in this way, vibrational pathways that create patterns which manifest in the way of crystals and lifeforms, or invisible energies like moods and behaviors. Knowing this we can understand these fractals as set designs of subtle energy, propagated into the conscious world as portals from which we both draw and contribute, an ongoing interconnected exchange.

286. A totem pole collapses and a new one is built

A legacy has collapsed, a tower of story has crumbled, one rendition ends and another begins. Though the pole itself has fallen down, it remains intact as a historical record with a wealth of artistic meaning. The stacked symbols show a tribal narrative, an inimitable legend full of animal totems and spiritual transcendence. We can study this depiction of what happened before as a preamble to our own unique tale as we erect the new totem pole with a fresh start. Having this clean slate there is a chance to take creative control, recording our own chronicles in the way we choose to retain them, elaborating only on what we wish to preserve, veiling other necessary truths or secrets in symbols, perhaps eliminating some altogether. As we filter our experience we are able to extract the highest significance from each epoch of our lives, and from this point of clarity and strength we build a sturdy foundation that turns into a grand monument of creative ascension one image at a time.

287. A belly dancer hands sea shells to a crowd

Bathed in femininity we are captivated by this rhythmic rapture as the grace of ecstatic woman enchants the crowd. With practiced control and elegance the belly dancer embodies the ultimate expression of woman's vitality, emphasizing her womb and her capacity to give birth, the sexuality of her gyrating hips, where fire meets water. As she offers sea shells to the crowd with her own hands, she incites a symbolic invitation to the watery seas of woman, arousing passions as the sounds of percussion and jingling jewelry lift us higher into the ecstasy. This celebration of sensuous woman mesmerizes us in the charm of her dance, where we are enveloped in the passion of female fire, energized and prepared to respectfully receive the shell she offers as access to her oceanic bliss. The source of all life, the heat of desire, the sacred feminine at her very highest.

288. Roses grow up around a cross

The representation of a cross carries broad implications as a symbol of life and death, its vertical axis a connection from the earthly to the celestial, opening interpretations for resurrection and the afterlife. As a four directional compass it signifies a totality emerging from one common center, corresponding to the human heart as the middle of our own bodily cross, the eternal symbol encoded in our fleshly form. This cross has been in place for some time, its long-standing mark receiving the gift of life as the roses crawl up and around it, blessing it with beauty and renewal of life, protecting it with its thorns. The heart of the cross sanctified by the roses asks us to align with our own heart center to receive this benediction for the sake of our life or another's, or perhaps an integrated love that includes both. The life represented in this cross is perennial, the beauty of the rose infusing everlasting spirit into everything it stands for.

289. Fruit sap drops down layers of trees

Bountiful trees are dripping with surplus, hanging fruit oozing out of their skins begging for a taste. It is time to harvest now as we enjoy the sweetness of the ripened fruits, while those beyond consumption are tilled into the soil as fertilizer to feed the tree again. A complete and attentive clearing creates space and cleanliness for future crops to thrive, as any invasion of colonizing insects attracted to the sap can devastate the entire trunk. In this same way, we clear ourselves of all that is messy and ready to rot, removing the mental debris and all of our decaying attachments. We share the bounty and enjoy the last sweet tastes of what is soon to expire, pruning our own beings as we drop the weight of overripe distractions that waste our vitality. Once relieved of this sticky mess we will be perked up and revitalized for our finest future harvest yet.

290. A religious expedition is led by a torch into the night

A spiritual passion calls us into the night to follow this luminous flame through the darkness. Where we would otherwise fall blind, this torch illuminates our path in the same way a deep faith eternally glows within to guide us, an inextinguishable spark of divinity inside each of our hearts. As we merge this sacred internal fire with our devotion to the highest holiness outside of ourselves, they are no longer separate. This is the religious expression of our expedition tonight, as we celebrate the divine light so bright it can pierce any veil no matter how dark it might be. We voluntarily step foot into the blackness of night to discover the essence of the guiding light that asks us to follow. Tonight we have a chance to feel for ourselves this fire of pure faith that leads the way when darkness falls, the source of heavenly salvation, the immortal flame of our soul.

291. Burned desert feet are relieved by a boulder's shadow

Conditions have demanded a temporary pause, we are invited to rest our weary feet in the natural shelter of this boulder's shadow. Relief is provided by something already on our path, so we need not veer off course to find rest, nor should we quit our expedition altogether. We need only to open our eyes to the reprieves offered along the way, astute enough to notice them and wise enough to honestly gauge our capacities in each given moment, knowing when to push ahead and when to fall back. However many more miles it requires, however strenuous or hot or painful it gets, we must move forward, and conserve our energy to resist overextending ourselves to the point of injury or exhaustion. Wherever we are, whatever we are doing, a refreshing break is offered in the immediate reach of our natural environment, asking only that we relax, cool down, and give in to this momentary pause.

292. Women trade strings and beads

In addition to the string and bead work itself being a craft, these women also embody artistry in the way they trade, diversifying their supplies as each one shares what she has to offer, a weaving in its own sense. Within the exchange their spirits are also intertwined, as the beads and string from each woman represent her own tastes and artistic inclinations, availing an accent to the otherwise usual creative leanings of another. This collaboration gives each of them a more varied assortment to work from, whereafter their creative individuality is expressed in how they weave the pieces together, intricacies of knots and beadwork, patterns and color that all

196

combine to form the unique rhythm that vibrates from any true work of art. We are inspired to refresh the supplies of our chosen craft, preferably by receptive sharing with fellow enthusiasts, a time to expand our material and add a spirited twist to our customary sets of design.

293. Lovers taste dew on the morning grass

The lover's embrace draws a sensuous arc from night to morning as the sun moves over the horizon. Rising together with the light they awaken in the dewy dawn soaked with love, the essence of their passion saturated and one with the morning meadow. Tasting of the verdant grasses slicked wet with dew, the lovers are refreshed in this mysterious ether of damp morning. We transport into this magical realm of sunrise, and with the delight of dewdrops on our tongue we taste the elixir of sacred morning. Whether with the beloved or alone with ourselves, we awaken radiant with a sweet glaze of sensual bliss, an immersion in our own ambrosia as the most natural etheric spirit of love. We absorb as much as we can as this nectar seeps from the atmosphere and pours into and out of our hearts, a kiss good morning, everything rich with passion and brand new, the dawning of a never before seen light.

294. A woman mixes water and clay

The woman's spirit moves through her hands as she shapes the clay into a form that will solidify when the moisture evaporates. As water carries attributes of sentiment and feeling, this fluid state of change is emotional, qualities that will soon stabilize into the earth in which they are set. Fortunately, this malleability lies within our creative control, so an eye for detail and awareness of the energy we imprint into the work is imperative. We have the ability to work our own beings in the way of clay, smoothing out our rough spots and blending in the emotions, giving us the chance to reshape ourselves into who we want to be when it all dries out and settles. This is an opportunity to become our own work of art, with all the beauty and flaws, remembering that personal power largely lies in how we take things into our own hands, the spirit by which we shape whatever material we hold.

295. A rainbow hits glass and turns into prisms

Such a spectacular display shows the intrinsic complexity of light, its colors dispersed into this wondrous view through many prisms. There is an inter-dimensional aspect to this image, as the initial rainbow is itself a prism refracted by an original source which then strikes this glass medium and further bends the light and breaks it down into multiple prisms. This phenomenal vision moves us to contemplate the nature of light and how, even though we normally cannot see it, that it still in fact contains the entire color spectrum. How awesome that ordinary light with a slight shift of angle can produce the rainbow, always there but usually hidden by the limitation of our sight, blurred as white light. May we gaze at this wondrous display with awe, imagining ourselves in the likeness of light, our own colors ever proliferating in all we exude.

296. One's eyes turn inward and they can see

Knowing oneself, being able to objectively turn in and observe ourselves, is a seminal component of self-improvement and inner peace. The human experience draws our senses outward to participate in the material world where our self-conscious ego seeks recognition and acceptance. Though this is a normal human condition, we optimize our life if we work to break the tendency to over-prioritize sensory perceptions which distracts us from a clear understanding of who we are and who we want to be. By witnessing ourselves and learning to track our mind as we notice our emotions and what provokes them, we can go inside and perceive a genuine self within. Here we find the integrated self as the unbreakable spirit, our true nature that only we ourselves can see, and see it we must!

297. A big leaf holds a pattering of water

We are zoomed in on this single leaf, and though it is big, the small pattering of water calls attention to detail. We hone our focus on one part of the whole forest, the distinct serrations of this individual leaf, its color and size and what it says of the tree from which it hangs or has fallen. Absorbed into the rhythmic sound of the patter our concentration naturally deepens as our usual thoughts soften and fade into the background. As our mental activity changes scale it moves into the specifics we usually overlook, the little things too often skimmed over as tiny nothings. With this ability to still our minds and dissolve our focus into small serenities, we train ourselves to easily move into a meditative space. Refined by this habit we discover great peace as we begin to tune into the endless tranquilities freely strewn through our world, as with the delight of pattering water on this perfectly unique leaf we would otherwise pass.

298. A fox enters new territory for the first time

This fox has crossed into unknown land, where caution and confidence must guide the exploration. The fox can be cunning on his hunt or quick prey himself, so knowing when to seek and when to hide must rule his judgement until he becomes familiar with this terrain. Our first instinctual impressions when we enter a new place reveal an intuitive truth about whether our surroundings are friendly or hostile, and as the newcomer in unfamiliar territory we are vulnerable. The nature of the fox teaches us the skill of cleverness to outwit our enemies, to slink and remain sly if we must be disguised, and to explore our environment with a coat of beauty and confidence as we sniff out this new world. Just as the deep wild instinct of the wandering fox will tell him when to continue on and when to settle, we can listen to our own inner guidance, trusting our earliest clues to tell us when to stay, or when to leave.

299. A magic woman turns into flower petals as she walks away

This ephemeral vision is a free flowing femininity, the elusive and transient woman with her soft folds, one with these fragrant petals as she diffuses into a mystical ideal beyond physical form. The enchanting woman exists outside the boundary of space and time as a magnetized cluster of conscious energy that spirals in and out of being through the essence of magic, a lucid sentience unrestricted by the body. Qualities as these are dreamy and vague yet paradoxically it is because of this vagueness that we are able to work with it. As a liminal image we can use our imagination to fill in the void, using the power of visualization to make it whole and meaningful to us. Herein lies the power of the sorceress who knows how pull images out of the ethereal and translate them into organized concepts that can be relayed into the physical world of our understanding. In seeing and living beyond the barriers of superficial form we gain a deeper vision into the subtle energy of everything, the true nature that lives beyond the illusion, the beauty of the magic woman.

300. A chained up man is released

The weight of penitence is lifted, the freed man is given the chance to start again. Even if the prisoner was tied up by his own reprimand, he is no longer confined to wallow in his shame. Whether the guilty verdict is cast from society or by our own infliction, it is time to unlock the manacles, the heavy chains of doom castigate no longer. A lightness has emerged that liberates the captive to embark unshackled onto a brand new path of freedom, transcending the memory, habit, betrayal, or self-sabotage that led to imprisonment in the first place. Having learned our lesson, however harsh it may have been, we must find love and forgiveness within ourselves to be cleared of our troubles and avoid running into them again. Unbroken by the hardships and failures, we stand proud knowing that our errors and misfortunes have made our character stronger, this once difficult time giving us wisdom that backs us as we move forward onto a clear path that allows us to rediscover ourselves, unburdened and free.

301. Dark birds peck into the earth

These dark birds are messengers between worlds, the iridescent blackness of their feathered wings signifies a magical ability to fly into other realms. As they peck into the earth they rouse what prowls beneath, exposing a hidden layer, pieces of prior times, their taps and songs and clucks further inciting lingering consciousness to stir. A spiritual channel is open, and with these mysterious birds as our guide we tap into the underworld, where lines of communication are open to ancestors and forgotten fragments of ourselves, providing a deeper access to face our fears and retrieve lost parts of our soul. This bird visitation is a magical charm to accompany us into the depths of our own dark journey, whether we are haunted by a ghost within or outside of ourselves, or if we are grieving a loss or wish to connect to a spirit in another realm, we follow these dark wings as they rummage through the pit and show us what buried remains are asking to be uncovered.

302. People draw symbols in the dirt with their toes

This barefoot play in the dirt demonstrates timeless joy and expression of the human spirit, a communal celebration that invites each individual to contribute their own personal symbols to the spread. This temporary art costs nothing and produces no waste, a carefree inscription that allows us to represent the elements of our personality that we wish to portray to other people and impress as declarations to the spirit of the earth itself. We notice the symbols and images by which we are identified, how we introduce ourselves to society in this tribal manner of understanding, using pictures rather than verbal explanations so that we can readily see our kindred spirits and our roles in the group. Sooner or later these marks will fade, the images will be carried in the winds that sweep them away yet live on through the eyes and minds that have seen them, perpetuating the living human spirit that collects all of our individual expressions together into one great archetypal story.

303. A pure spirit is born and a demonic one dies

As all universal wisdom understands, there is an eternal power struggle between goodness and malevolence, yet both must exist to generate any living motion at all, as one without the other would cause everything to fall flat. The distribution of these energies play out in the mysterious origins of the cosmic unknown and influence our behavior on earth, determining trends of consciousness and world events. We feel the wide reach of these forces inside ourselves, as even the slightest whispers of evil tilt the scale of our being as do small acts of goodwill shift the balance in this constant fight. This is a tip towards goodness, a diabolical energy is exchanged for a positive influence, so we too banish the evil entity within and make space for this pure spirit, a benevolence is born.

304. A group of masters meet the true master

This gathering of masters shows that supreme mastery is never conclusive, there is always someone more accomplished, even if it is the fulfillment of our own future potential that awaits us. Each one of these masters is at the top of their local order yet amongst other leaders they become the average as the standard is raised in the presence of the true master. The highest master knows the work is never done, there is no finish line that grants a definitive top status. The pursuit of mastery is ongoing, a ray of continued perfection that always ascends, a line of progress that begins somewhere but has no point of arrival. If we improve tomorrow, we will be the masters over ourselves of today. With this we make an agreement to walk a higher path, to practice and advance each day for the rest of our lives, the endless quest of the true master.

305. The ill are soothed with barks and boiling water

The purpose of any remedy is to reharmonize an unbalanced condition, the antidote being the opposite energetic quality of the problem. The heat and volatility of these boiling barks as the effective solution indicates we are counteracting a stagnant chill, a lethargy that requires us to rev up our circulation and speed up our metabolism. We are cured through detoxification as we sweat and purify with this soup, an astringent that soothes our ailments as we rest while the medicine works, after which we slowly increase our activity to rebuild our energy. This hydrating medicine dislodges the source of our malaise, and freed of our troubles, we are warmed up and balanced, vital once again.

306. An uninhabited island goes underwater

The island is swallowed by the sea, a reminder that time never stops and from the microscopic to the galactic, things are always changing and moving through an active process. Everything in existence is dynamic, actual stillness is impossible in the temporal confines of our world. Nothing, not even the ground under our feet, is set forever. Each moment slips slowly into the past, and anything can wash away suddenly and completely with surprise at any given moment. Rather than sinking with the fallen earth and drowning in anxieties over such notions, we notice instead that the island is uninhabited, a contemplation that offers an alternative mindset. In the wake of the eerie waters where the landmass just sank, we hear the pervading wisdom of its absence. The island was empty, no life was lost, the consciousness was only somewhere else.

307. Children skipping rocks on a lake

There is a delicate skill to spinning these rocks, a certain twist of the wrist to make them skip, and as they breathe in the fresh lake air, the children are engaged in a healthy combination of practice and fun. As each stone is unique in its form, so too is our every toss and all the ripples they create, this metaphor of nature aligning with our own lives. Even our body rhythms correlate with the earth as we immerse in this play, the water with our blood, and the stones with our wrists and bones, the organic world integrated. By tuning into the best of these living moments, we satisfy our lifelong need for connection to nature as we open our hearts to reverberate with the universal beat of everything. When we release into these natural

205

rhythms, we merge with them, harmonizing with nature's forces as we develop more finesse and control over our every gesture, every rock that we throw.

308. A lush pond with algae and croaking frogs

Ponds are stationary waters where tranquil life may bloom, an indication that fertility and abundance is presently found in a placid place. There is no rush, no current, only a stable body of water as its own lush ecosystem, quiet but for the croaking frogs announcing their readiness to mate and settle in this thriving habitat. As with all bionetworks, the success of the resident species is dependent on their mutual survival, the interconnectedness of the pong largely sustained by its great algae that provides food for the surface dwellers and protective cover for aquatic life. As we reflect on the prosperity of these peaceful waters, we take note that our immediate fecundity is found in undisturbed stillness, where we rest calm in our own pond of inner tranquility. With this focus we relax into the joy of the singing frogs and let the bustling life around us roll on, quiet for a time to sit still and soak in the rich pool of our own serenity.

309. A clairvoyant benefits from a séance

The beneficial séance indicates that attempting contact with the dead could be advantageous to us at this time, if not by ritual then at least by invocation of memory followed by concentration so that we may hear what the conjured spirit has to tell us. We are told it is specifically the clairvoyant who benefits, so this is a call to awaken our telepathy and tune into our extrasensory perceptions to commune with a wandering spirit, even if we access only a piece of them that lives inside our own hearts. However we attempt to reach our chosen contact, if we can tap into our own clairvoyance there is a promise of internal reward after spiritual exchange in this communication with the dead.

310. A vampire drinks blood and then dies

The vampire's lust for blood has backfired, the wrong prey was pierced. Whether killed by holy contents of the blood itself or by divine intervention as immediate retribution, something has slayed the ruthless predator. The downfall of the cold blood-thirsty parasite shows us that the good and the innocent are protected, the vital blood of life pumps through the image steaming with a warm, heart-filled essence strong enough to pound a stake into the heart of evil. We sanctify our plasma, our blood, the life force that beats through our veins to fortify our strength of heart and will, to keep pure faith flowing through us so that any evil that reaches for a taste will find us spiked with a holy resistance that will defeat anything, a conviction so pungent that the greedy bloodsuckers will fall at their first sip.

311. A god makes an appearance for his people

A beloved deity appears in this miraculous benediction, the highest blessing conceivable for any faithful follower. This visitation presents the ultimate mystery as the manifestation of God, a divine unveiling that tells us to take a look and see this higher power for ourselves. However we praise this supreme source, the merit of our faith is assured in this revelation where we encounter exalted divinity. Once we reach this summit and clearly visualize our object of worship, a deep sense of love and peace will flood through us, a confirmation that someone or something is there to answer our prayers and shine a guiding light, an omniscience beyond the scope of our understanding. This appearance is the great reward and continued promise of persistent faith.

312. A flock of birds lands in a park for scattered grains

Public parks are waystations where civilization meets nature, a place for flocks to gather, of people and birds amongst flowers and trees. Contrary to the wilderness where wildlife must fend for itself, the park attracts all sorts of local life with various offerings, scattered grains to feed the birds. The park is a small pocket of the natural world where animals lean more domestic and society leans more wild, an intersection between two worlds. Feeding the birds invites them to descend for the joy of the people and the satisfaction of the flock alike. In the peace of the park we contemplate the flocks, those of birds and those with whom we fly, recognizing motivations to land and what we ourselves choose to swallow from the spread. We notice as well our own hand that feeds, and what sustenance we contribute to the masses, both in society and nature, what we offer to the shared park, where multitudes of life gather and exchange.

313. A bridge is built from two sides

A rift is bridged making each side equally accessible to the other so that shared ideas and middle ground are now possible. The ends that formerly flanked the divide have made an alliance and agreed to cooperative communication, a pact that has the mood of a truce. Successful construction of this bridge requires a mutual effort from both sides to meet in the center so that the unifying structure is durable and resilient against collapse, thus a strong keystone of reciprocal support must be our foundation. How often the bridge is actually crossed is the decision of each traveler, but accommodation and openness have been avowed in this undertaking.

314. Numb walking souls come to life

These trapped souls wandering around in catatonic bodies have been spared their atrophy, a coldness cast away through an oomph of life. A deadened vacancy that had plagued these apathetic pedestrians is filled with warmth and passion to live, a new vitality circulating through them as they are restored into full cognizance. Liberated from this comatose state we can stimulate our own numb lodges of forgotten feeling with this flush of vigorous energy, an exhilaration that opens the floodgates to purge indolence. Awakened by this new stamina, we walk forth with explicit lucidity so that nothing may dull us down from this resurgence. As long as we stay alert and continuously engage the pieces of our soul we do not want to waste away, we will prevent the downfall of prolonged inertia. Resurrected from complacency, we receive this burst of fresh life and walk on, our souls animated, fully alive.

315. A high mountain peak where spirits take form

This aspirational ascent lifts us into the clouds and onto the summit of a sacred mountaintop where the world axis touches the divine. A holy moment of tranquil stillness, we journey into our meditation and rise with these spirits on high, and with our bodies at peace on this crown of the earth we float freely as our own spirits join them. As we drift into this mountain serenity, we dissolve into the place where heaven meets earth, the threshold of divine exchange where we blend with these spirits of present manifestation, merging with those we wish to receive and return with as a part of ourselves. As long as we continue to visualize and climb such great peaks, heaven will greet us at these majestic heights where earth turns into sky, where physical bodies consort with boundless spirits, our highest point of truth where we undulate breath with pure source, selecting spirits from above to inhabit our earthen body below.

316. Deep in the wilderness a solo explorer draws on cliffs with charcoal

Exemplary qualities of human nature range from our wild curiosity to our intelligent use of language and the arts, both praiseworthy attributes of this explorer. Alone in the deep wilderness, the courageous adventurer discovers and marks upon the cliffs, expressing a present rendition of an ongoing story as personally observed in this unique coordinate of space and time. The cliff itself tells one geological tale, and the charcoal as a charred firestick reveals its own burnt history as the traveler sketches out a personal interpretation of the moment to inspire and instruct forthcoming travelers. As we trek through unnamed lands into distant edges never tamed, we enter places unknown where we attune with our uncultivated wild selves. In solitude we seek to explore these faraway depths that await our discovery, a blank canvas of expansive cliffs spread high above us where we may pick up the chalky black remains of the fallen past, and reach to express our story from the wide vista of this present moment, the way we want it shown to ourselves and anyone who follows in our footsteps.

317. A rich meal is cooked after a sporting victory

This culinary indulgence is well deserved after a hard earned victory, the athletes and chefs alike celebrating the successful demonstration of their craft. As any champion knows, excellence in a chosen pursuit is the result of the highest dedication and tenacious training, commitments that paved the way to this winning moment. The warmth of the fresh meal is cooked with esteem for the love of the sport, a double satisfaction that fortifies all participants with abundance and joy, a time to lap up the sweet taste of triumph and savor the riches of our reward. We lean in and surrender to the full flavor of this delicious acclaim, soaking in the delight of each bite as we honor and celebrate the exuberance of our success.

318. A rebellious spirit rejects her pre-prescribed path

Willpower and free choice have taken a stand over the restrictive expectations of others, the imposition of false dreams is decisively rejected. The strength of such defiance opens the way for our personal visions to authentically manifest without the pressure of unwarranted compliance to follow destinies we do not choose or by becoming beholden to fraudulent limitations that try to stop us. This rebellious spirit thinks for herself, believing in the inner direction that lives inside of every individual, both as loud calls within demanding inspired action, as well as the quiet whispers of heart wisdom that tell each of us what we can only know for ourselves. A spontaneous arousal of faithful purpose is born within, a genuine freedom sets us onto our rightful path as we embark on the distinct journey of our individual destiny, led by the guidance of our own autonomous will.

319. A lone wolf howls at the moon

A call of the wild, the lone wolf sings into the great expanse of night, a primal howl amplified by the moon. The mystical moonglow serves as a transcendent light that receives this sound of the soul and bends it into the realm of spirit. The resounding continuity of the drawn out howl evokes the loneliness in our own hearts, projecting it into the emptiness of the likewise lonely sky. Far-reaching and bold with wild instincts, this signature of solitude fills the shared sky to place our present state of being into the context of a wider existence. The wild nature of this illuminated night invites us to cry out our own emotions, to sing our messages of longing, to express our role to the distant pack in any way we wish. As the howl of the wolf echoes within the deepest chambers of ourselves, our true soul song emerges and flies free into the open night, across the sky and into the light of the moon, where the spirit world beyond is certain to hear it.

320. An ecstatic woman rises into the sky

A blast of bliss skyrockets this woman out of her body and into the sky. Her feminine energy has shot from the earth, ecstasy has catapulted her into the heavens, and completely taken in supreme rapture she soars higher yet. Attuned to this boundless female power we realize her sacred intuitive energy is the portal of all desire, the pure essence of pleasure and live-giving creation, and whether sexual or maternal, she is the refuge for our deepest longings. Pleasing and serving the feminine within ourselves or our loved one, or any goddess to whom we are devoted, ignites this powerful ecstasy that by nature must surge into the sky and then settle back down in an auric afterglow, this kundalini arousal as the full cycle of ascension and descent that will activate and sustain our highest union with the divine. Her terrific bliss inspires us to feel the coiled energy spiral that rests at the seat of each one of us, the base of our flesh that yearns for ascension, searching for what lies beyond the body, delivering us to a euphoric epiphany, an elation that is sky high.

321. A band of thieves rides wagons in the night

Beware of these thieves creeping around in the night, with wagons of loot rolling on quiet wheels travelling in lightless disguise. These robbers on the run are methodical in their slowness, inconspicuous and skulking along to their next mission, an unexpected theft sure to catch the victims off guard. Secretive and sneaky, the vagabonds on the move may go anywhere, so with this tip we remain stealthy ourselves to avoid becoming their next target, also wise to not draw attention to ourselves or anything we hold of value at this time. With one eye open we remain watchful, vigilant to prevent theft of our possessions or ideas, or even pieces of our soul wrongfully taken by bandits in the world of dreaming or by subtle energy vampires in our everyday lives. However these thieves pass through our province, we protect our belongings and hold our contents of self a little tighter, remembering these gangsters are not a band of bombastic raiders, but a cooperative calculating group that steals from us when we are off guard and sleeping.

322. A generous family hosts greedy visitors

Generosity is noble and needed for the common health of humanity. However, if the generous overly give to the greedy they are at risk of depleting themselves of the supply that grants them the ability to give in the first place, inevitably draining the time and resources reserved for others in need, both now and in the future. From the perspective of the visitors, they must learn to accept graciously when receiving kindness, to express gratitude and reciprocate as possible, maintaining self-awareness to avoid the greed that leads to unhealthy dependence and avarice. As either giver or receiver of anything, we must strive for balance on both sides of the equation, recognizing any surplus we can afford to share while honestly gauging where we come up short and might benefit from the support of others. When in balance, gracious receiving and generous kindness together create a mutual human support system that harmonizes our struggles and perpetrates goodness and sharing in the world.

323. A man and a woman carry logs to a wood stove

Working to prepare the stove with the support and company of a partner stokes a natural bond. This warm cooperation lightens the load for each of them while creating an ambience that enhances the entire experience. The eventual reward is their mutual enjoyment of the fire, its comforting heat and potential to cook food, among the greatest of all enchantments and sources of necessity and joy. Once we light the flame, the fire requires steady attention, a balance to ensure we fuel its persistent need to burn while also remaining aware of its all-consuming capacity for destruction if left untended. The present fire is so far nurtured with care, the gathered wood contained by the metal of the stove, a sincerity of thoughtful awareness felt in its preparation. The nature of the image bestows its continuity upon us as we carry the energy of the flame forward to our own sacred vessel to excite the warmth of our own passions. We kindle a comfort within ourselves that appreciates the willing partner, two who together light this naturally vibrant yet peaceful flame.

324. A long scroll unrolls with a never before read story

A novel story unfolds. There is a new tale to be told in this revelatory message, an inscription certain to surprise us. With high anticipation this original manuscript will soon be revealed, teaching us something that until now has been kept secret. As with any new account, discussions will be roused and we will ponder the content in our own minds, the way quality knowledge is meant to challenge our thoughts and broaden our limits of understanding. Full of themes

215

that adjust or affirm us, we are impressionable to a skillful narrator's perspectives and ideas that suggest new ways of being and interpreting life so that we can better understand ourselves. The long scroll indicates a dignified communication, one to thoughtfully decipher as its time has ripened for this present disclosure. Previously hidden, the virgin scroll is an honor to witness in its unveiling and we should be receptive to this epiphany of sacred words.

325. A hardened person softens as they break down and cry

Suppressed feelings have finally released as they are wept away in this river of emotion. Until now, this hardened person had been locked out of their own emotional world, frozen in a detrimental desensitized state of apathy and cynicism. Now the block of ice melts down in this freefall of tears as we simply let go. Here, even the toughest person is called to cry without inhibition. Sobbing, or at least freely venting out our words from time to time, wrings us clean of built-up pain and frustration, of our difficult emotions and the burdens we bear. Whether alone in private or with trusted support, our spirit has refuge in this moment to soften our breath and sigh, to let it all go as we break down and cry.

326. A sweep of bravery inspires a coward to take a daring quest

The coward finally notices an inadequacy in themselves as a source of their own misery. If we identify our deepest fears of failure and ineptitude, the restrictions we self-impose to avoid humiliation and rejection at all costs, we open up to the sweep of bravery that rushes in to conquer it. Called to the daring quest we have the opportunity to crush the cowering dread and disprove the illusionary shortfalls that steal our potential. We boldly step forth beyond the reaches of our habitual comfort and look the nature of the problem straight in the eye. Determined to rise above this inhibition we banish our despised weakness once and for all. We return from our quest with a determined mind and confidence in our voice, standing tall and proud…tried, tested, and true.

327. A lion outruns its enemy

The majestic lion shines in semblance with the sun as the king of the wild, golden rays emanating from the waves of his mane. Faithful to a pride yet solitary as he pleases, the lion is the apex feline of power and courage, streaked with solar gleam as the emblem of a fierce and vital heart. The lion outruns his enemy in this race for survival, the heartbeat of victory pounding as he escapes attack. Tapping into the deepest wells of strength, the brave lion shows us that the heart is not a generator of anxiety that forces us to flee uneasy, but a source of mortal valiance. As we absorb the solar rays, we soak the courage of the mighty lion into our own hearts, and wild we run strong, triumphant and pursued by our enemies no more.

328. A mother finds her lost child

The separation of mother and child is dramatic, especially if the young one is still dependent for their basic needs. If it is an older child who was lost, this resolution may be more emotional and less weighted with trauma, though in either case the reunion is intense, restoring the most fundamental relationship in all of existence. This event emphasizes the significance of the maternal bond, and whether we are mother or child we are invited to reach out to the other on a meaningful level, by voice or spirit, by apology or forgiveness. We reestablish our love for the mother, or any origin from which we've drifted away, as we likewise rediscover the love for our children, for all we tend and all we create as nurturers ourselves. Creator and created renew their bond in this revival of mother and child.

329. A hungry bear emerges from long hibernation

The dormant bear awakens from wintry quarters after an extended rest, slow-moving and ready to eat. After such a long hibernation it will take some movement to warm up the blood and wake up the nerves so that the muscles can function and the bear can return to full activity. Emerging alongside the bear, we stretch and blink open our sleepy eyes, ready to look upon the world again after this necessary rest. This prolonged withdrawal was essential for replenishment of self and the resources that sustain us, the recent season having been naturally cold and unproductive. Such a long spell of stationary dreaming has allowed us to conserve our energy while the subconscious was able to journey without interruption. Free of distractions we are now cleansed and settled, emptied and prepared to begin again. With a healthy appetite we emerge from the dark cave to search the world of plenty, motivated to build ourselves up again as we step into this long-awaited morning of fresh light.

330. The subtle rise and fall of the heart is observed on a loved one's chest

The intimate depth of an honest love inspires this deliberate observation, the subtle throb of the heart rising and falling under the flesh. The tender eyes of true love take us into perceptive study of the living pulse as the closest possible look into the heart of another, beyond the superficial. Our affectionate gaze leads us deep into the beating rhythm of the loved one's vital essence where we see the pumping life force in motion as a signature of the soul with whom we long to connect. Dissolving into sensual appreciation of the other we secrete the nectar that flows with poetry and love, we drink it in through the lover's eyes that ride the contours of skin by the dance of the pulse, a connection that infuses the surface of the body's bliss with the depths of pure heart, the most naked expression of love.

331. A group chants and prays and it all comes true

The spoken word is immensely powerful, especially when chanted in rhythmic repetition as a declaration of intent, even further amplified by the contribution of a group. Every sound we emit is full of vibrations that transmit thoughts and feelings from our internal existence to the outer world, a means of asking and receiving inherent in all we assert. Anything we create with our voices forms a coherent container of energy outside of ourselves, attracting to itself what will sustain it as it harmonizes with the external conditions that support its development. All we express, everything we chant, the meter and intent and quality of each sound, ring through the universe as a tone that will echo back to us in the likeness of spirit by which we ourselves proclaim it. The vibrational fields we tap into with prayer or mantra or any kind of chant reach into the dimensions of divine mystery, where our passions are heard in this faithful song, and resonant with our deity we praise them today. Our prayers have been answered!

332. Night bugs fly into a candle and die

All life on earth organizes around the daily cycle of the sun, each sunset a signal for the creatures of the night to rise and come alive into their waking world of darkness. Informed by light or the lack thereof, the insects are misled by the candle as an unnatural occurrence, and thrown off by the false direction they crash hard and fast into the flame. Without a firm orientation of where we come from and where we are headed, the warmth of the glow and the fascination of the fiery flicker can entice naïve wanderers to fly straight into the center of the heat where its power incinerates in a flash. As a foolish pursuit can distract our rightful way or a faulty spirit may lead us blind, any imposters of truth can misguide us with the temptation to follow a false light. We wise up and take a careful look before we proceed towards the allure of this spark in the night, first gazing from a distance so that we may witness what the light illumines and what it destroys before we ourselves fly into the fire.

333. A small space in the earth rests a weary traveler

The earth is our home. From the dust of the earth we come and into the earth again we shall return, and to it we are connected in every step we walk. At rest we sink deeper in as its rhythm lulls us to sleep. A weary traveler is called to refuge in this alcove of the timeless mother who welcomes us all into the basin of her womb, this bowl of earth. Cradled in the repository of minerals and silts, we accept our smallness and with full peace we drop into the earth as our deepest sense of existential home. This little nook offers us a respite, a place to curl inside and surrender to a comfortable rest where we can retune to the heartbeat of the living earth as our most organic relationship of true life energy and deep belonging.

334. Willpower forbids an insistent parasite

An invasive entity is trying to latch onto us, a persistent parasitic force has been grasping. Though we have forbidden these incessant attempts from direct attachment, it has still taken energy to fight them off and we must continue our vigilance until the threat is gone. To use the willpower that defies this encroachment we need precision of mind to locate the areas on our bodies and in our lives where we feel drained, the sites of the parasitic entries. We check ourselves, noticing anything that feeds from our vitality, whatever leeches us and leaves us depleted with no replenishment in return needs banishment now. It takes willpower to cast this force away, so however microscopic or biological, however dominating or human or spiritual or subtle, we must slice it off with the clean cut of a psychic sword, and redirect the energy to flow inward. Rather than allowing it to leak away, we return this nearly lost vitality back to ourselves.

335. A book of knowledge illuminates a seeker

A single source of illumination provides the present answer for this aspirant. The seeker has found guidance that inspires new light, a revelation of an enlightened way of thinking or being. Now that the orientation has been set and the spark of knowledge is lit, the real work begins. We are challenged to remain dedicated, as once the initial enthusiasm wears off, there can be a tendency to prematurely think we've mastered something when we've really only just begun our course of study. If we abandon our illuminations too early, we prevent any real depth or meaningful application of the subject to our personal evolution. If we are devoted to an ongoing study and focus, however, we have the opportunity to develop a central channel of knowledge and wisdom from which everything else branches, a main line that supports us into limitless growth and discovery. An entire life study could begin with this single book, one that is ready to lead us onto a path to find the answers we most seek.

336. A strong force suddenly collects many magnets

An electromagnetic field has been incited, a polarity has asserted its extreme charge into an otherwise stable zone, stirring up sudden changes. This gravitation is attractive and compact, many magnets compressed into a tight central pull of great magnitude. An impulse of such scale generates a chain of reactions, first as a compensatory

222

energy that resists the enormous pull. Anything with the opposite charge as that which flows towards it is repelled and deflected outward with equal force, both forces then further influencing all other fields that come into contact with this massive energy path, series upon series of electric switches turning on and off. We consider the impetus, what signaled this surge of magnetism and what lies at the core of such an attraction. Once we sense the essence behind the pull, from where the source of its energy lies, we can make a conscious choice of how much we want to open up to this powerful current, setting up resistors or conductors that alter our own charge, determining how easily we are pulled towards or pushed away from this sudden aggregate of extreme force.

337. Behind a dark veil a dark elf nature spirit guards a secret pond

The secret of this pond is double buried in darkness, occluded behind the veil of night as well as by the supernatural protection of the dark elf guardian. Sacred places tend to have mystic shields that protect them from unwanted interference, filters that prohibit offending energies from coming too close. These can be thought of as mysterious conscious entities that share our physical world, functioning and living simultaneously alongside us but operating from other dimensions, planes partially overlayed upon our own with different angles of projected form and light that we cannot see. Only those who can see through this hidden veil of darkness will find passage to the secret pond, access to its waters only allowed to those deemed worthy by the guardian as the dark elf nature spirit. This enchanted glimpse into a truth unseen calls for respect to all precious places, a reverence for the sacred and the supernatural watching over everything.

338. A storm destroys a house but it is built back stronger

The inhabitants experienced a tremendous loss when their house was ripped away by the surprise of the storm, the entire foundation of their security destroyed. However, the event has passed, the home has since been rebuilt and now stands even stronger than before. Between the catastrophe and the resurrection there had to be a period of recovery and hard work, a time to process the loss and cope with its difficulties. At some point, resilience was chosen over defeat and a plan was made to move forward in a realistic way with attainable goals, challenged yet certain to stay strong and steady in the wake of the mighty storm. From the rubble of our devastations we pick up the shattered pieces and with fierce determination we set forth to build something even better than what we had before, our homes of house and self both reinforced, unshakable and ready to withstand any storm to come.

339. An orphan learns meaning and heritage

Lacking a direct living relationship with natural parents, the orphan is intrinsically prone to experiencing a sense of abandonment, left without meaningful stories of origin that others are secured to as familial roots. As this orphan shows us, however, there is a beacon of hope, a feeling of belonging and heritage can be discovered by anyone regardless of bloodline involvement. This acquisition of meaning could be information about unknown parents or identification of part of the lineage that lived prior to them. It could also be a newfound fit as a part of a new family or tribe that welcomes us in to share a part of their story as our own. With this adoption we develop a deeper understanding of our place, a legacy bequeathed as an ancestral awakening that sheds light on a bigger story, a continuous stream of meaning through time, a heritage of which we are now a part.

340. A large first harvest from a sacred garden

The sacred garden is one held with the highest respect by the loving hands that touch it, the thoughtful gardener putting intentional energy into all that is sown, a consideration of each sprout, the continuous nurturing of every plant as it matures to harvest. Monitoring the moisture and nutrition of the soil, using organic methods that build up the land rather than deplete it, and attention given to the most sensitive things like the words spoken and moods emitted from the hands that tend it, all contribute to the sacred approach of growing the beloved garden. The bounty of this first harvest sets strong the sacred garden's name, showing us that with intentions of highest love and respect we can plant powerful energies into the inception of anything we wish to hold holy, a veneration that if sincere will flourish through the entire cycle. As we enjoy the harvest we feel the love return to us, an energy from which we can spread the seeds again, in the garden as well as in other areas of life, and as future seasons pass, more and more, we learn to nurture the sacred in everything we love.

341. A cobra slides between two thrones

The slithering cobra twines around two thrones, weaving them into a knot of new knowledge, a renewal of wisdom and rule. A seductive force with venom in its jaw slides as a secret mediator between the two seats of monarchs, a potency of raw creative energy meandering beneath their feet, informing every decree of law and spirit. With its sly successions of sliding throughout the thrones, the cobra implements its power, winding and unwinding a fundamental serpent knowledge ever slipping by us and through us, one that guides this royal rise, informing the highnesses on the throne whether they know it or not. When seated on high, it is imperative we are grounded enough to see the beguiling snake that lurks beneath, sure to differentiate the deadly strikes from the ones that wield wisdom and power so that we are aware of the source of the forces that guide us into this period of inspired rule.

342. An old man and old woman stare at each other wide-eyed

Time freezes as this old man and woman lock eyes, a captivating awe transpires in their stare as if they are really seeing each other for the first time. A profound stream of love is palpable in their gaze, the openness of the wide-eyed stare feels as though they are bearing naked their souls. There is a mutual recognition of longevity and experience, a beauty made deeper by the endurance that gave space for trust to grow and appreciation to build. Whether this couple has been together for many years or they have just now met, there is great meaning in this soulful exchange, an immersion of inimitable connection in this fully surrendered stare. The look riffs with the contentment of familiar surprise, exemplifying the reward of viewing life and our loved ones through a new lens each day, allowing growth and maturation to always fascinate and maintain wonder for life and the other. Beautiful the mirror flows between long-loved eyes, swirling together into a truth deepened by time, the golden fleck on the iris that just now appeared with the rise of a fresh smile.

343. A lovely woman caresses her own skin

A personal ritual of self-love and wellness keeps us feeling healthy and beautiful and connected to ourselves. The lovely woman is radiant from her own caress, a deep sense of acceptance and happiness instilled and enlivened by her loving touch. In the subtle patterns we trace and the neural paths we consciously and unconsciously explore along our own skin, we tune into an intimacy that only we can experience in our own body, a positive relationship with ourselves vital for our well-being. By massaging ourselves and caring for our bodies, we tend to our emotions and release somatic burdens, brightening our skin and our aura into an energy that is loved, and therefore loving. We emit positive emanations that exude health and beauty, the appeal of a confident glow that harmonizes us first with ourselves and then with what we attract with the call of our light as self-love shining.

344. A spiral makes a black hole in the sky

This spiral winding through the sky has become so dense that it
has compressed into a black hole, a vortex of contained energy from
which nothing can escape. As it gathers more pressure in towards its
center, the vessel seals entirely and in reference to what is outside of
it, disappears from sight and understanding. As the coils of the
moving spiral tighten, its circumference decreases, and its projected
direction becomes more certain as it zeroes in towards an endlessly
precise center. Since we cannot see the black hole in the sky, we are
challenged to view the spiral from the inside and imagine the intense
power of its whirling contents, and like a fine-tuned telescope we can
align our own visions with this narrowing optic that opens a portal
into infinity. We live in a nebulous reality, a truth all of us may
imagine, yet none of us can know, so imagine we must.

345. Escaped pearls gather on the ocean floor

Anything on the ocean floor requires adventure to find. Only a
plunge into the unknown will take us there. These collected pearls
are lost but not forgotten, that is unless we ignore them and let them
drift deeper to sea. Each pearl is an accrued jewel of wisdom in its
most precious form, every one with a unique reflection of knowledge,
together an assortment of experience and insight that transcend time,
yet with one small slip can flow away, forever lost. We hold our
treasures close and keep them above water, sharing them only with
those who appreciate their value so they are not diminished, piled in
with the ordinary, buried under sea. To preserve the opulence of the
shimmering pearls we must drop into the deep basin of ocean and

return the forgotten to the light of the sun where their luster will illuminate again, a rediscovered brilliance sanded clean, ready to emerge in this next wave of renewed life.

346. An old elk lays down to feed a village

The elk has lived into old age and the time has come to lay down its life. A generous spirit seems to oversee this natural death, a feeling of sacrifice permeates as the elk lays its enormous body down to feed the village. Eternal energy is always travelling from one life form to another in myriad and complex ways, simple in the way that everything must eat other things that once lived, and the more elaborate realization that we also consume the sum of all energies impressed into everything we eat. As the elk rests peacefully into the earth, serenity is imbued into the entire process, a lack of suffering and a well-ripened life leaves a positive energetic current in the body left behind, which will in turn transfer to the village people who eat it, as well as into the spirit of the elk. If we observe the sacrifices all around us with gratitude, infusing respect into all things that feed us and everything we ourselves offer, we churn positivity into the universal energy shared by all life, a vital exchange ever pulsing beyond the reaches of life and death.

347. Exiled people find some place even better

People flee their homeland, whether by force or by choice they are exiled, in pursuit of a new place. Turning away from what they have known, feelings of rejection or betrayal are sure to arise, as well

229

as fear of the uncertainty of what lies ahead, not to mention the difficulties of the expedition itself. Despite how it might feel at first, however, we know that this relocation is the best move. In attempting the chosen risk, or by tolerating the inevitable, the journey proves successful and there is a real chance for reinvention of self and story in this fresh start. If we or someone we know is at the threshold of any form of exile, we trust in the timing of this escape, knowing a good outcome awaits us when we arrive at this better place ahead that is waiting to welcome us home. Hoping for acceptance and smooth integration into the new community, we remember to leave the parts of ourselves we wish to escape behind us and bring the best of ourselves to the surface so that our good fortune continues and we find meaningful belonging in this new land.

348. A dark phantom of night breaks into the day

The blue sky of daytime is slashed open by this phantom of darkness. A sudden emergence of shadowy gloom breaks into the light, a dark presence descends onto the day. We cannot look straight into the sun without going blind, nor can we touch it, but the dark phantoms we can face without a blink, we can in fact walk right through them. Formless ghosts are deliriums of errant energies, remnants of conscious beings, fragments of thoughts, elusive hauntings that slip through us, or may even be of us. The invisible composite of dark energy, the black cloud, the inexplicable arrival of heaviness or despair, may have broken into the day, yet the day persists. With the filter of darkness we can better gaze towards the light behind it, staring right through the phantom until its invasion is

230

shunned by our recognition and it rescinds back into the dark land behind the sun, leaving the day bright and clear for us once more.

349. Artists pound and chisel sculpted bone

This artistic endeavor is an ongoing commitment, as another layer is detailed beyond the vague shape already sculpted into the bone. Bone being a substance of strength and durability, there is a possibility of long-term appreciation for the piece if it turns out well in the end, a motivation to make the work truly exquisite to honor the artists as well as the spirit of the animal who provided the bone. With the availability of these sacred materials and the right tools we know we must show up to complete this important work with full dedication. We look at the chisel in our hands and gather our quality supplies, the roughed out blueprints we are ready to carve out and advance into the next stage of development. It is time to be particular and distinguished in our artistic signatures to dignify our work, cutting no slack for shortcuts or laziness. Techniques and skills made interesting through the unique creative eyes of an artistic spirit is what generates amazing art, so we welcome the muse and concentrate on finesse as the next phase calls us to focus our efforts and let loose the power of our own highest creativity, an offering solid as bone, certain to last.

350. Women fix feathers into each other's hair

Women rise together in this ascension of beauty, the plumes of the feathers lining their hair as they elevate each other in this uplifting and supportive atmosphere. Their spirits turn airy and light as they decorate one another with feathers, goddess adornments as free birds flying. The lightness by which they ride the sky beneath their wings lifts their smiles as they take on the higher spirit of the bird's knowledge and power, their songs of free joy soaring as they float on their toes in this dance towards the sky. When women cooperate and rise together, their shared blessing enables them to ascend even higher, naturally ecstatic and flying feather high, the core celebration of every woman. Let the woman we are or the woman that we love, our friends as the women all around us, each be seen with her hair as feathered wings ever flying, and encourage her to rise, rise, rise!

351. A high domed ceiling hosts echoes of sermons

This lyrical cathedral rings potent proclamations, the spacious dome bounces the sermon through the heavenly heights overhead where we sense a divine touch resounding the importance of the message. As these powerful teachings echo inside the dome, the entire structure booms a marvelous truth, the congregation resonant with the strength of its vibration. A soul revival is alive in this chorus of words we witness, the transmission is prophetic and poetic and reverberates as a rhythmic revelation of celestial ceilings, everyone within the echoey chambers carried into this elation. An epiphany of spirit is sounding, the refuge of sacred space calls us to look high up into our own sanctuary of inspiration, where we listen and receive the teachings that echo in harmonious melody with the gospel of our own truth.

352. A child breaks through an icy lake but lives

A quick pang of shock has shivered us to the core, but the chill of the bite averts death's grip. The frozen lake snaps open with a crack of ice and the child drops into the waters, but survives the close call. We hear the icy break shatter open a fragile truth, tender and conditional is the flesh itself as well as the reality knowing that what appears as a sturdy block of thick ice can turn out to only be a thin sheet ready to collapse at the slightest touch. When treading untested waters we might stomp out a few steps ahead before putting our full weight down to make sure the surface does not buckle under our feet, remaining ever ready to hop back if the stability over frozen water begins to fracture. Like the unknowing child, at times we stumble or we take a wrong step, sometimes we are even plunged hellward and freeze in a momentary death, but even still we climb out of the pit. Once a warm-blooded body has felt ice in its veins, never again will slaps of little chills feel so cold.

353. The full moon illuminates an owl perched on a tree

From our geocentric perspective, the full moon is opposite from the sun in space, and with the earth positioned between them we are in the center of the strong magnetic pull created during this lunar phase, when all terrestrial energy intensifies. This is the fully expressed relationship of the sun and moon, a channel of light energy that focalizes a tremendous amount of power onto the lunar surface, and the moon reflects this potent force with great amplification back down to us. From the height of the tree, the owl in the spotlight receives this direct transmission, its own wisdom further illuminated

233

as it becomes a conduit for the teachings of sky and earth. The relevant wisdom of the present moment does not arrive in the plain sight of a sunny day, but glows in the night as a knowing that requires us to seek out the moonlight and bask in its beams. Accompanied by the wise owl, we step out to the darkness and climb onto a limb, and perched over the shadows we tune into the present lunation, receptive to the convergence of universal wisdom perfectly aligned to illuminate our way.

354. A mystic has her first psychic vision

The mystic is validated in this revelation of her destiny, her authentic connection to psychic phenomena confirmed by this initiatory vision. This event opens her to a path of further development, where she may refine her metaphysical senses and intuitive perception so that she becomes a consistently reliable medium of oracular insight, a rare gift that can help the spiritual and human dimensions interact with one another, linking them together with a pure cord of communication. This idea inspires us to listen to the cues of the universe, the subtle vibrations before something falls, the clusters of energy we deeply sense telling us to look further into what some might dismiss as pestering thoughts, realizing these are in fact the directives of fateful spirits trying to convey important messages. If we stop and look, listen and feel with more sensitive acuity, we will begin to perceive with more depth and prescience, and whether we relate to being a mystic or a psychic or not, we will more closely resemble what it means to be one.

355. Confidantes whispering secrets in each other's ears

These words traveling through quiet careful lips are certainly not public or expository, rather they are intimate and private, the whisper heard only by a single ear, anything shared arriving with the warm life of the speaker's breath. We appreciate the close quarters of the confidante, someone we hold in great faith to protect our secrets and in turn trust us with theirs, a closed exchange that forms a distinct bond, the lips so close to the other's ear, a vulnerability in the softness of the speech, vocal cords exchanged for whispered exhale. This is a time to invest social energy in our closest confidantes as a source of support and motivation, only broadening the pressing questions and disclosures at hand to a wider circle if and when appropriate. What is internalized often needs spoken, and without oversharing we tenderly whisper into the ear of a confidante, who with our best interest in mind can take some of the weight from what we hold inside, a support we offer as well to our dear ones in return.

356. A distant war recedes and the residents cheer

Peace abroad is peace at home, any war that ends is good for all life, minimal suffering at the core of our common human hope. We see the resolution cheered on in the celebration of these distant residents, taking us to another part of the world to peer into their conditions, the horror of war giving way to peacetime. As the devastation of combat subsides, there is a new appreciation for what is often taken for granted, the great luxury of feeling safe and at peace. The relief of the residents gives us a rush of gratitude for peaceful times, the blessing of every day we live in the absence of fighting and fear. We can join the celebration of this populace in this moment they break free from war, and harness the triumph in our own lives, releasing the tension with our own adversaries, peace treaties offered so that both sides of strife can live harmoniously once again. The winds of compromise are in our favor, we make truces with our enemies and forgive the warring we impose within ourselves. The aggression is receding, a ceasefire underway, and a glorious renaissance is waiting just ahead.

357. A victory speech that inspires as champagne is poured

The human spirit is profoundly moved by inspired articulation of gifted orators who can touch the core of the soul, who can synthesize big ideas into meaningful phrases and share them with charisma. This victorious speech spills forth as the champagne pours to celebrate this transference of wisdom absorbed together in common company. Motivation flows into the group through this crafted message of eloquence and value distributed through the attendees as each of them piece together their own unique understanding of what they hear. When the triumphant and brilliant isolate the keys of success into palatable kernels that can be widely applied through various types of people, a victorious society is in the making. In this light we strive to imbibe the wisdom of learned experience shared all around us, while also extracting the keynotes of our personal wins so that we may transmit them in a useful way to others, and herein we participate in the continuous flow of inspiration to enrich ourselves and the world around us.

358. The sounds of celestial bodies become pleasantly perceptible for a brief moment

The pleasant perception we presently enjoy is an audible anomaly, a sound normally out of range. As multitudes of celestial orbits swirl through space, they vibrate in various frequencies that combine to create light and sound, spirals as concentric galaxies intersecting and curving in and out of torus shapes and worm holes and other perplexities, all held together in harmonic resonance to maintain the fabric of existence as we know it. Our senses can only perceive a minute fraction of this cosmic symphony, a complex interaction of ongoing patterns built into all structures of form and movement contained in the entire universe, including the intervals between musical notes and the steps of ascension within scales and octaves. We briefly fuse with another dimension in this harmonic overlay as an otherwise imperceptible celestial music slides into our sphere as a galactic gift, a serendipity of great scale as we rise into this heavenly octave and absorb the sacred chords, a numinous resonance we can forever carry like our favorite song.

359. The hot ash grows a secret flower

The residue of heat smolders as ash, fire energy active but subdued as it settles onto the earth. Incineration of the wood and other raw material has broken down the structure of its prior form and transfigured the matter into an altered substance, its essences recombined to open energies for a new purpose. Nutritive properties have been drawn out from the burned plant matter now concentrated into the ash to foster the growth of this secret flower. This

237

alchemical process shows us that the fires ignited within and without aggregate the release of potent components inside the base material, separating the refined extraction and liberating it into a transcendent power. Once a form dissolves, when anything runs its course, a piece of spirit remains, and sifted down to its vital base it remediates the blossom of the secret flower, dormant until transmuted by the hot white heat of the fallen ash.

360. Lead turns to gold

This is the grand alchemical transformation, the great work of an entire lifetime, the observation, modification, and refinement of ourselves through this process of transmutation. Beginning as an amalgamated mess, we identify and separate the leaden impurities, the pieces that sicken and stall us, removing ourselves from all that has happened to us, burning away the dead matter to reveal the untarnished golden essence of who we really are. We've worked hard to assimilate our experiences and polish our heart energy into a perfect center of wholeness, and now aligned with the universal equilibrium that organizes all energies and elements into a harmonic cohesion, we have built our astral body as the great golden seal of the self, our incorruptible aura of congealed light, the most precious substance in the world.